W9-BRM-472

5/16

Coyote Settles the South

Coyote Settles the South

JOHN LANE

The University of Georgia Press ATHENS

FREMONT PUBLIC LIBRARY DISTRICT
1170 N. Midlothian Road
Mundelein, IL 60060   WITHDRAWN

A Wormsloe
FOUNDATION
nature book

© 2016 by the University of Georgia Press
Athens, Georgia 30602
www.ugapress.org
All rights reserved

Designed by Erin Kirk New
Set in 10 on 15 Minion
Printed and bound by Sheridan Books

The paper in this book meets the guidelines for
permanence and durability of the Committee on
Production Guidelines for Book Longevity of the
Council on Library Resources.

Most University of Georgia Press titles are
available from popular e-book vendors.

Printed in the United States of America
20   19   18   17   16   C   5   4   3   2   1

Library of Congress Cataloging-in-Publication Data

Lane, John, 1954–
  Coyote settles the South / John Lane.
    pages cm
  Includes bibliographical references.
  ISBN 978-0-8203-4928-2 (hardcover : alk. paper) — ISBN 978-0-8203-4929-9
  (ebook) 1. Coyote—Behavior—Southern States. 2. Coyote—Habitat—
  Southern States. 3. Lane, John, 1954– —Travel. I. Title.
  QL737.C 22 L 255   2016
  599.77'25—dc23   2015032666

For Drew

"Being a genius certainly has its advantages."

[notices lit fuse, dynamite explodes]

—Wile E. Coyote

Contents

Prologue REDEMPTION SONG

The coyote is a coyote anywhere you find him.

—J. Frank Dobie

We first heard them behind our house in upcountry South Carolina on a warm Halloween night after we thought the trick-or-treaters had passed. My wife, Betsy, looked up from reading and said, "It sounds like the hounds from hell out there."

Standing on our back deck, we listened. The predictable stirrings of October on the edge of our upcountry suburb swaddled the evening—lingering insect thrum, a slight wind rattling the autumn leaves, a neighbor's dog barking. Then it started again—a tumult of high and low yips and whines. I tried to locate the source of the foreign sound, but all I could see was a smudge of dark trees and a commuting plane with blinking red and white lights passing in the southern sky. I listened again to a chorus of mottled voices from two directions, only a few hundred yards distant.

"What is that?" Betsy asked.

"Coyotes," I said. And then, like the little blond girl in *Poltergeist*, I added, "They're here."

Our place has no shortness of wild animals. There are minks, beavers, muskrats, otters, and raccoons in the creek and floodplain behind our house, and we've seen them all. Betsy has even glimpsed a bobcat on a walk at dusk along the creekside trail. On several nights I'd once seen a gray fox crossing the road near our house, headed back into the floodplain. A wood duck raised a brood in a hollow oak nearby; Canada geese honk over each morning and evening on the way to and from their foraging on the local golf course; and a pair of red-shouldered hawks once nested in a large oak practically in our front yard.

There are tiny ring-neck snakes in the flowerbeds and a resident black rat snake or two, and a persistent population of king snakes feasts on them all. Betsy likes seeing the mammals and birds, but the snakes are a harder sell. She says they give her the creeps, so I don't always tell her what I've seen or where. I definitely kept my mouth shut when a large red-bellied water snake took up residence in our small frog pond outside the bedroom window.

One afternoon walking our beagle, Murphy, we saw a four-foot copperhead coiled on the edge of our backyard. I called a herpetologist friend I teach with, and he caught the snake with a set of large aluminum tongs. It was an old snake, the largest he'd ever caught. He studies the movement of copperheads in the wild, and he wanted to plant a transmitter in it and return the snake to the floodplain, but we decided against our wild yard serving such a science experiment.

We live in the suburbs, but I have always been comfortable with nearby nature. In my mind I inhabit a dream republic, a cross between Ernest Callenbach's 1970s utopian novel *Ecotopia* and the television show of my childhood *Wild Kingdom*. I like the people who live nearby, but I need wild animals as neighbors too, and I've always known a landscape calls for something even bigger and fiercer than the secretive bobcat Betsy saw. What we needed was a top-of-the-food-chain predator in the big woods behind our house. It was inevitable. We'd be lucky if in our lifetime we could see black bears on the edge of our backyard, but instead, the coyotes surprised us with their arrival.

But not everyone likes a healthy mix of wild and domestic. Far west of us, coyotes are a species *Homo sapiens* like us have been at war with for more than one hundred years. It might not be any different here.

Just this morning in the local paper a teaser photo on the top of A-1 featured a coyote trapped in a county below ours. I looked closely. A deep terror flickered in that coyote's eyes, but there was also a fierce will to live, a stoked-up fire of survival. Its mouth was wide open in defense as the photographer approached. Its teeth reflected all the suburbanite Goldilocks fears the fairy tales play on. "The better to eat you with," those who look at the picture might hear the coyote snarling, fangs bared.

Something is pornographic about the local paper's willingness to publish a photo of a trapped animal. The paper wants a quick emotional reaction. It wants fear to sell like a tonic. I'll admit I was pulled in, party to their smut. I turned the page to read the story. The same photo was repeated in a smaller version at the top of the Upstate section. The title in bold print called coyotes a county nuisance, and the lead offered a rural dweller's absurd complaint. The coyotes kept him up at night, so he paid a trapper to come catch thirteen of them on his property. One of them is in this photo, dead soon after the camera snapped. Now the man can sleep at night. The story plays on dark fears. The coyote might eat your dog or cat. The coyote is definitely eating the deer local hunters should be shooting. The coyote might snatch your child, might even eat you.

After we heard the coyotes that first time, the sound became our nightly music. Three weeks after we first heard the yips and barks, the first classic coyote howling began. They rang high, quivering cries strung through space like a clef of ascending notes held too long, a little lonely, but with a strange beauty. The howls were intermingled with the familiar ensemble of spooky yips, but it was the howling that filled the dark space of trees and water below the ridge with a dense sonic mystery.

Sometimes they'd sing early in the evening after sunset, but mostly we'd hear them deep in the night at three or four in the morning.

Often a distant siren would trigger the ensemble of high-pitched coyote barking. Other times they'd open up for no discernable reason. The males, I learned, were the ones with lower tonal range, the females higher. Some people have compared this choir of complaints and grunts and yips and yodels to violins in smoothness; others say it sounds like more animals than the choir ever does, each individual at a slightly different pitch of song.

Hearing the nightly sounds of the coyotes created a complex reaction in me, part curiosity, part what E. O. Wilson calls "biophilia," a love for the living world. After hearing the first choruses, I read whatever I could find about wild canines—popular natural history books about wolves by Barry Lopez and Rick Bass, books about mostly western coyotes by Hope Ryden and J. Frank Dobie. Soon I knew that many who have pondered the lives of the canids start with their hunting, but sitting on the deck, I first imagined them tending a nearby, dark productive den. I preferred settlement to describe these coyotes' arrival, and I imagined a pair of them moving freely up and down the floodplain on the edge of our suburb looking for the best suitable real estate for their family, digging a burrow, maybe altering and lengthening gaps in piled gray concrete edging abandoned in the construction landfills across the river, or finding spots where berms of hardened red clay block sight lines from dirt access roads, or where errant boulders are cantilevered into rock shelters, and dumps of piled oak stumps trucked from suburban construction projects form warrens of air pockets, and clots of dirt dangle like pendants from the ceilings of these inaccessible spontaneous caves.

From my perch above the southern woods, I pictured this pair of neighborhood coyotes slinging fresh dirt behind them in winter, adding right angles to their entry tunnels so that no one but they could enter, and then for months later, circling back to where their newborn pups waited to suckle. My eyes need the light, unlike theirs, and so in reality, it was only in my mind's eye what goes on where the sun never shines. To really enter coyote family life I would have had to dig them out, so instead I simply conjured smells clinging to and swaddling boulders and rubble. I constructed what softness the cool earth offers, conforming to the bodies of the returning adults (for both male and female tend the litters), what sounds were emitted by the small, downy snowballs born with floppy ears.

It was even harder for me to imagine the pups huddled in their dark, secret winter dens when their tiny eyes open at ten days and their ears grow erect the first time. With a little more reading I learned a litter can contain anywhere from one to nineteen pups, but only half of them likely will grow to adulthood. At three weeks (here in South Carolina, maybe in January) they would emerge from the darkness and begin to explore the neighborhood outside their den. At five weeks they would be fully weaned, after which both parents fed the pups on regurgitated food, quarry killed and scavenged on hunting forays.

It was easier for me to imagine these coyotes as mysterious young adolescents. At six months (in early summer) the adolescent males would leave the den to explore, and the young females would stay behind, forming the basis of the family group. Autumn is when the new generation would venture out to establish territories of their own, to live, but mostly to die. Both males and females, if they survive, reach full growth and sexual maturity at about a year. They are observed as tawny-coated teenagers dispersing, spied from deer stands, from speeding cars, eating pears in October from a suburban tree planted in a backyard, appearing suddenly in midday across the street from a downtown car dealership, glimpsed at a street's end on the outskirts of the old Victorian neighborhood a block from the town square. They circumvent camera traps and snares, recognize individuals who want to harm them, and learn to avoid tree stands; they raise their young, they hunt, they move like wild night marauders through our neighborhoods and yards, like special ops teams with the best GPS receivers in their pockets, out for an easy mission in the woods.

Coyote hate is a common theme of Facebook posts, hunters' chat boards, and news articles, and coyote fear is growing across southern cities and the country. But I don't hate or fear them, though I know they can be dangerous. Nationwide, in the time I have been following the story of coyotes, there have been dozens of coyote attacks and at least one death. At night when I hear the coyotes in three directions and the serenade goes on a long time, it occurs to me that there is no sound more American than this, a coyote howl, and so to hate it (and them) is to hate myself.

Now when I hear the coyotes howl and yip, I always put aside my computer or book or worries and crank open our windows, or crack the door, for however long it takes for the floodplain to pass into silence again. You could say I am attending to the songfest of wildness on the edge of our suburb. I even turn on a small recorder and enter the latest canine cantata into my inventory of aural encounters. I listen to these recordings over and over and play them for friends as if they are part of a wild symphony I need to acknowledge, like the latest pop song.

I've listened long enough now that I believe I can sort out individual voices. I am really hooked, over the edge. These canine cousins have become real to me—individuals, beings with the rights and privileges of presence. They are no longer abstractions.

A month or so after we first heard them, I had my first face-to-face encounter with a real southern coyote. After we heard the music, I was determined to see one, so I walked every morning down to the creek with Murphy. Finally, one morning I looked down the trail, and trotting away from me was a single coyote, downwind about a hundred yards distant. Coyotes can be grayish brown, like the one I saw, or even yellowish gray, and sometimes black, while their throats and bellies are often a buff or white. Their forelegs, sides of the head, muzzle, and paws are reddish brown, backs tawny with long, black-tipped guard hairs that can form a black stripe on their backs and even a dark cross on the shoulders. The coyote I saw saw me as well but simply looked back and maintained a leisurely pace down the trail. In that first brief coyote encounter I saw some promise of wildness returning to our region. I saw the redemption of our landscape wounded and scarred by hundreds of years of human settlement, a hope that may be hard to explain to my friends and neighbors.

Or maybe the wildness had never left us, was with us in some altered form. One night as I listened to the coyotes, Murphy awakened from sleeping on the couch and tuned in as well, and I wondered about his perspective as a domestic dog, the most successful of the canines. As Hal Herzog puts it in *Some We Love, Some We Hate, Some We Eat*, "Hooking up with odd-looking and hairless creatures was a strategy that worked out well for *Canis lupus familiaris*." Murphy's girth and comfortable spot on the couch only underscored Herzog's point.

Murphy was tuned to a frequency more ancient than his kind. Domesticated or not, his ears are often alert, the edges slightly erect and ready. In his wrinkled brow I could see a little confusion. His eyes showed uncertainty. Would he join this chorus unsettling the night air or simply listen? His wolf ancestors parted ways with coyotes a million years ago, and yet here they were, together again. Would he join the sing-along? Only recently did coyote and dog genes start mingling again, as coyotes pioneered eastward and wolves and dogs added some genetic baggage to the canid inheritance.

"Murphy," I said. "They would eat you in one gulp. You would make a good coyote Happy Meal." After a moment or two, Murphy joined in the chorus, curiosity (or genetics) more powerful a pull than fear. His response was full of passion, but maybe slightly off key with the surroundings, as he greeted his new neighbors singing for life in the floodplain below.

Now that the coyotes behind our house have settled in, I ponder Mark Twain's pronouncement of them as "living, breathing Want." I have my own human desires. I want to encounter them, to understand the outline of their presence in my suburban backyard. I want to understand—if possible—what it was they want, and thus I embarked on a project to see the world both from my point of view and theirs. Immigrants from elsewhere, do the arriving coyotes simply want to settle new territory? Or do they want more? Do they want only to hunt, to eat, to mate, and to breed? They are here now, but will they stay around, and if so, what will my—and by extension, our—relationship with them become?

Scatology

To follow on the track of fish, birds, or any other animals,
might be both discovery and repetition, because it might
mean to go exhaustively into the nature of being alive.

—John Hay

In January the coyotes were back. I'd picked up six separate samples of scat on the trail behind our house. I'd even used Murphy to help find the scat. Murphy kept his beagle nose close to the ground as we walked. I had never thought of using my dog as my own personal scat detector until I read an article about a researcher in New York State who trained her Labrador retriever to seek out scat and sit beside those left only by coyotes. It sounded like a good idea, so I watched Murphy closely, and sure enough, he walked off the trail to pinpoint three deposits in the dry leaves I would have passed right by. I even took to carrying treats in my pocket so I could reward him each time we came upon these signs.

Why care what's shitting in your neighborhood? Because each deposit is like a book waiting to be read. From what's left behind it's possible to find out what your animal neighbors have been eating. Scatology is a little like going through the garbage cans lined up on the street on pickup day. The first time Murphy led me to a deposit of coyote scat I picked up a twig and poked through what he had found. Four inches long, the scat was pinched at one end. First thing I noticed was that my defecating neighbor had been feasting on late-season persimmons. The shiny cinnamon-colored seeds clogged the dark brown deposit.

Once I got into the scat project I made an intricate map of the series of trails in the corridor of woods behind our house, and I numbered each intersection, one through six. When I found a deposit I placed it in a plastic baggie, and with the Sharpie I carried in my pocket I logged the location, date, and weather like a scientist.

Unlike a scientist, I knew that I would not carry through with any research. The scat would likely sit in the plastic baggie for a week, never worked up, hairy with mold. Instead, it would function as an image in this story, a prop, a few lines in a paragraph. If there was coyote "research" to be done it would have to occur on foot, from the seat of my pickup truck, on the trail, the experience carried back and processed later out of a notebook, pulled from the plastic baggie of my own skull.

In late January I walked along Lawson's Fork behind our house. The trail was through bare winter woods. I was walking with my friend Mike Willis. Mike used to be a trapper, so I guess you could say he's retired, though he's only in his mid-fifties. Following us was my Wofford College colleague Gerald Thurmond and fifteen of his interim students. Gerald's class was spending the entire month in search of animal signs, utilizing a series of morning meetings and hikes to learn the world of scat and signs.

Gerald is a sociology professor. Mostly what he teaches is social psychology, gender, and the family, but the college interim classes give Gerald a chance to tune up on the natural history he practices. We take these walks in the woods for many reasons—love, curiosity, and a range of other emotions and drives that are only half understood. Neither one of us has the connection to the wild world that Mike has, though we both wish we did.

The American archetype of the trapper runs deep. The image of the mountain man alone, dressed as an Indian, wading in deep snow, his horse heavy with sets of traps, has been celebrated in western novels like *Mountain Man* by Vardis Fisher, and films such as Sydney Pollack's *Jeremiah Johnson*, starring Robert Redford. Mike's been trapping on these trails behind our house since his boyhood days. I always wonder what he sees as he walks through these woods. I know he sees signs and tracks we don't see. I wonder if he sees any portents that might lead me to the coyotes I seek? What would happen if Mike turned his attention to the coyotes behind our house as I have done? Could he catch them? Could he track them along these trails and set traps for them and bring them to me?

For me, walking the trail behind the house was a triumph of sorts. Two weeks earlier I had broken two ribs (one in two places) in a fall at home. As I walked I realized that the accident was my first true encounter with a different sort of coyote spirit than the one analyzed in all the scientific papers about coyotes I'd been reading. This time coyote serves the purpose of the trickster, and the powerful figure had a field day with me in early January. Coyote is out there somewhere in mythic space, laughing.

On a Tuesday morning before the hike, I'd been answering emails in the living room. Betsy and Murphy were sitting side by side on the couch. Suddenly Murphy looked like a Gary Larson *Far Side* cartoon, "How dogs throw up." He stood, stiffened, and began a familiar arching of his back, moving the contents of his stomach outward through a series of rhythmic retching upchucks we'd come to recognize quickly. You know how dogs hurl—one, ugh, two, ugh, three, ugh, then—blah!

"Get him out! Get him out!" Betsy had said, in a panic, pushing Murphy off the couch in the middle of the process.

We'd been through this drill many times. The dog would head toward the dining room rug where he'd let it go. I was to intercept him, pick him up, and head for the door where I'd toss him on the deck. Everything happened fast. I picked him up and held him out front. I was not aware that he'd already completed his sequence and the puke was in my path. I hit the dog vomit and my feet flew out from under me. I went down hard on the corner of a built-in bookcase next to the door, and the dog landed on all fours in front of me.

When I hit the bookcase I knew from the pain and the movement in my back that I'd broken some ribs. I couldn't get a breath. For a moment I thought I was dying. After I was gone, how could Betsy possibly explain to anyone that dog vomit had been my undoing? "Relax and you can breathe," Betsy said, and she was right. My breath came back, but the pain was excruciating, and I couldn't sit up.

After an ambulance ride and six hours in the emergency room, I was finally back home with painful ribs, a bottle of Lortab, and a volumetric spirometer. "Blow in this ten times an hour," the doctor said. "Broken ribs can't kill you, but pneumonia can."

For four days I couldn't walk from one end of the house to the other, much less a mile. The injury didn't stop me from thinking about coyotes. Outside each night at about nine, they mocked me from their sanctuary deep in the floodplain. Their song served as a Greek chorus to my misery as I played my spirometer flute. After ten days I finally felt good enough to drive my truck downtown, stepping gingerly on pavement when I parked.

Not being able to travel far from home after the injury, I focused on the woods I walked through, the bare winter oak and hickory thickets climbing the eroded hills north and south of the creek, the net of birdsong suspended around us in the last cool of midmorning, the thin sandy soil of the floodplain, and needle sharp of the green smilax vines.

As Cormac McCarthy's novel *The Crossing* begins, all the deep accumulated wisdom of trappers has disappeared, along with the very trappers themselves. The hero of the novel, Billy Parham, and his father have to remove a wolf from cattle country of New Mexico in the days before World War II, so they go to the locked-up cabin of Echols, the departed master trapper of the territory.

McCarthy describes the cabin as like a magician's chamber—"a strange basilica dedicated to a practice as soon to be extinct among the trades of men as the beast to whom it owed its beginnings." Inside

Echols's shuttered cabin Billy's father forages among the abandoned, stoppered essences of the lost trapping craft: "the dark liquids. Dried viscera. Liver. Gall. Kidneys. The inward parts of the beast who dreams of man and has so dreamt in running dreams a hundred thousand years and more."

Later, Billy watches his father set the first trap and he thinks, "He looked to be tuning some older, some subtler instrument.... Like a man bent at affixing himself somewhere in the world. Bent on trying by arc or chord the space between his being and the world that was. If there be such a grace. If it be knowable." On my walks I too was trying to get as close as I could to my place's essence—like the content of one of those dark jars opened and exposed in McCarthy's trapper's cabin.

On the walk with Gerald and Mike, I took the point, and I worried a little about our loose organization. If we were a platoon of soldiers, I thought, Indians with bows and arrows could pick us off and the others would never notice. I've known Gerald for thirty years and I know he was not worried. He strolled at the back of the column, talking with Mike. I knew from past experience that an outing like that for Gerald was total freedom, and he liked to impart that freedom to the students. On some hikes he gets back to the cars and somebody's missing, and he just waits for them to catch up or sends out a search party if finally needed. In three decades of teaching in the field, he says he's never lost anyone for more than eight hours, so it must work.

I circled everybody up anyway. It gave me a chance to pause and rest my rib cage, to pass a little time until Gerald and Mike showed up. I told stories of the mammals we'd seen behind our house in the decade we'd lived here—a bobcat, minks, raccoons, deer, squirrels, rabbits, beavers, foxes, and now coyotes. I told of seeing the coyote on an early morning hike, how I spotted it in the trail twenty yards ahead of me, and how it simply looked back over its shoulder, saw me, and trotted on. "Oh," I say, "and possums," and I ended with a story of my encounter with a mortally wounded possum on the upper trail. "That bloody possum staggered up the trail toward me and then fell over and died right there," I said, just as Gerald and Mike walked up.

"Be sure to write in your journal that Professor Lane scared a possum to death," Gerald said, lingering with Mike at the rear of the line.

Along the trail, seasonal pools were full to the brim from the recent rains, and I knew they'd soon be densely populated with courting spring frogs. We'd hear them from our deck in the same way I now hear the coyotes. I paused to look at one of the pools. A large flock of grackles passed overhead, chattering away, and pulled my eyes upward. The students stared as the powerful surge of black chattering grackles moved just above the treetops as they passed. They weren't Carolina parakeets (now extinct), but it was still exciting to see so many birds.

After a while we stopped in a clearing in the floodplain where a large swamp chestnut oak claims all the available space above. Mike caught up. I prompted him to talk about the spot. His speech is deliberate, weighted with cadences of the local. He picked up an acorn almost the diameter of a quarter. "These are the biggest in woods," he said. "The deer come here to eat them. This has always been a good spot for a deer stand." Then he pointed out a deer stand on a nearby, smaller, sturdy ash. We all looked over to where he pointed and saw the rigging for a stand fifteen feet up the trunk.

"Me and my son Mikey bow hunt here," Mike said. "He's the fourth generation to hunt these woods."

We listened as Mike talked more about his life hunting and then about his past trapping on the Lawson's Fork, the small piedmont stream that runs behind our house. Mike looked around at the deep forest to the nearby creek. "I started hunting here in the sixties and seventies, and mink and muskrat were still plentiful. My uncle told me that in the 1930s he made somewhere between two and three dollars a day working downstream in the mill. He could get two dollars for a muskrat pelt, and seven or eight dollars for a mink."

Although Mike only leases the right to be there, he has the deepest connection to the place of anyone I know. "My grandfather told me stories about this place. He called this the Russell Bottoms," he said. "My father told stories of catching carp when they drained the mill-pond downstream. I shot my first duck right down there around a bend."

Mike had a career—"if you can call it that," he said—back in the 1970s and 1980s trapping minks, beavers, and muskrats mostly along this waterway and others in the county. "Then the bottom fell out of the long fur market. I turned to other things, like carpentry."

Trapping animals, for food or fur, has been with us for hundreds of thousands of years. As a profession and calling it's been around much longer than my preferred mode of communing with the natural world—the creation of essays. Long ago in the last Ice Age people trapped to acquire pelts to protect themselves from the cold. Today, people still trap all over the world for survival, sustenance, and money. In this country, trapping is now highly regulated by wildlife agencies, and state and federal laws set the terms on how, when, and what people can acquire in these ancient methods. But in spite of decades of harassment by PETA and other animal rights organizations there are still modern-day fur trappers in almost every state, though several states have banned the practice. Most commercial fur is now taken from animals raised on farms, and old-time trappers' numbers are dwindling.

Sears Roebuck and Co.—what we now call simply "Sears"—used to be one of the largest fur-buying companies in the United States. The store created a promotional booklet written by "Johnny Muskrat" called "Sears Tips to Trappers." Every week Johnny Muskrat narrated a radio broadcast called "The Fur Market." Beginning in 1926 all the stores hosted a National Fur Show each year and awarded prizes— even cars—to the best trappers nationwide. By 1959 Sears halted the show—and the fur buying. This was about the time when Sears decided to switch from a rural focus to the urban market. Mike's trapping started a decade later and somehow survived into the 1990s.

In McCarthy's *The Crossing* the wolves out west are described as smart, smarter even than all but the master trappers. They are actively engaged in the process of beating the trappers at their own game. Trapping becomes part of an ancient true prey–predator relationship. I think Mike would agree with this assessment of the relationship. He's told me how much he loved wading the creeks, summer and winter, to check his trap sets, sometimes a dozen up- and downstream of every bridge on Lawson's Fork. He's said he learned how to climb out of the creek, a rifle in one hand and a dead muskrat in the other.

Now he only occasionally practices his craft when he hires out as a nuisance trapper for corporate and private clients whose creekside properties have been inundated by beavers. I'm convinced because of his trapping he is closer to McCarthy's "tuning of some finer instrument" than the rest of us.

I've talked with Mike a good bit about coyotes. Unlike many of his hunting friends, Mike isn't that concerned with coyotes coming into this country. He's said that he's only seen them once or twice in all his hunting of the area—he is full of stories others have told him but doesn't have many of his own. "I stopped trapping before they came into the area," he said. "My friends tell me they're everywhere. Everybody seems worried about what they'll do to the deer. I'm not sure they understand the coyotes are here to stay."

Earlier in the month, before I fell, we'd talked at some length. I'd told him I was writing a book and wanted to see a coyote again, and he suggested I walk down to the shoals every morning and climb into one of his son's tree stands. Now I was limited in my climbing. "I think I'll come back here and just sit for a few hours right here on this river bank," I said. "I might see something that way."

"When you sit in a deer stand, you sit for four or five hours," Mike said, leaning back. "Time passes like a good movie."

When we reached the shoals I sat quietly and let my mind wander as the class explored. There were coyotes hunting this river bottom, and I knew that they claimed it for their home territory. I had so little to go on: a few piles of scat, some howling sessions in the night, and five hundred pages of academic reading that may or may not apply to the eastern coyote. Researchers have warned me that the habits and life-ways of western and northeastern coyotes may be the same for these pioneers, but they may not be. Southern coyotes may have adapted new strategies for survival in a new land. Only more research will fill in the gaps to what we know, but I still couldn't stop my imagination from wandering.

The slope behind me faced south and I'd read that up north and out west female coyotes looking for dens prefer these exposures, since they are warm to the sun through January, February, and March. I assume January and February is the time of pair bonding here as well, as it is up north, and a female and male coyote may have already been court-ing somewhere in the floodplain, forming the nucleus of a family that would stay together until early fall.

Because they bear only a single litter annually, the rituals of mat-ing are very important for coyotes. These canines aren't like Mike's muskrats, which can get things wrong because they have five or six chances a year. Much depends on this one matchup. When it's time, the females discharge blood-tinged fluid, going "into heat," and, much like many humans, the males and females take part in both aggressive and what the scientists called "affiliative" behaviors, or in layman's lan-guage, flirting.

I imagined them circling, tails up, yelping more than usual, the big male and the smaller female; I imagined the female running away in the winter woods, and the male chasing her like some furbearing Romeo hell-bent on getting his girl. Each stopped to urine mark. When she was ready the female would sniff or lick her mate, and even mount him, or stand with her tail twisted to one side. And then comes the copulatory tie or the lock, end to end, a trait as old as canines themselves, and one that frightened me as a child, a time when dogs in the South and everywhere else still ran free and mated in the streets.

Imagining coyotes mating in the woods around me isn't science, but it is half of what I do when I write about them like this. As Mike has turned to these woods, I hope to turn full-face to the coyote's story. The other half of my work came earlier, looking for their real presence, seeking their sign, something closer to research. Before I began to make my map of the coyote scat, at the trail intersections I picked up the first few dry powdery deposits I found and broke them apart in my hand and sorted through the contents with my index finger. Mostly I found the ubiquitous persimmon seeds, and mouse hair, and even once the tiny crescent of a mouse incisor, but once deep in one scat there were two small dry beetles the color of chocolate, and as I poked at them I wondered if the coyote had eaten them or if the mouse had eaten the beetles before the coyote had eaten it.

I know the coyotes are out there. Someday soon I would encounter another real coyote somewhere, but until then, these speculations and explorations would be the margin notes I'd keep on this new species. I'd content myself with their excrement. That was my evidence, how I'd make my map, how I'd know that something I do not see is my neighbor.

Coyote on the Run

And Nunn would hunt and hunt some more; all his
heart would go out to the hunting.—From *Hunter's Horn*,
by Harriette Simpson Arnow

I wanted to take another trip, to get out into the southern woods again, so late one evening in early June I drove an hour
northeast of Spartanburg and waited by the side of the interstate for
Richard Rankin to call. Richard had arranged to take me to one of
the last surviving hilltop hunts in the rural country north of Kings
Mountain, North Carolina, on Wade Ward's farm. In spite of what I
know about old-time rural hilltop hunting, that today it isn't so much
fox hunting as coyote hunting, I've never done anything quite like that
before. I'd read about a fictional hilltop fox hunter in Tim McLaurin's
novel *Woodrow's Trumpet*, and I'd even taught it years ago, but I never
thought I'd be out on a summer night experiencing the hunt.

In *Woodrow's Trumpet*, a man many consider the town idiot hunts
night after night, his hounds baying to the sound of his hunting horn.
In the novel's fictional moment, it's the 1980s near Chapel Hill, North
Carolina, and the suburbs are closing in around Woodrow. His hunt
and his hounds running free are anachronisms in the Yuppie New
South, and so is Woodrow. Woodrow's running of the hounds is
counter to the real estate dreams and rising property values of the
owners of the land around his four hilltop acres.

Twenty-five years further down the line from McLaurin's novel, I
still like the idea of old-time hunting traditions surviving in the rural

seam between the thick sprawl of Spartanburg-Greenville, South Carolina, and the even thicker sprawl of Gastonia-Charlotte, North Carolina, but as I sat and waited for Richard beside the interstate I felt a little guilty because I live front and center in what's making it so hard for these old-timers like Wade Ward to keep their rural traditions alive. As I sat on the side of the road I recited the factors that have essentially killed "running outside," and they made up a pretty formidable list: paved roads, and four-lanes in particular, suburbs, the return of the white-tailed deer and the deer culture of hunt clubs that accompanied it, and what I was most interested in, the coming of the coyotes. As I waited to be ferried deep into old-time hunt country I reviewed all four of these factors at work in the world of Wade and his friends. And yet the hunt survives, and the coyotes, by most indication, are much more plentiful than foxes ever were.

A few years earlier, long before I became interested in coyotes, Richard had visited a course I was teaching on the rural South. Richard's a headmaster of a private school up in Gastonia, North Carolina, but much of his passion and pleasure is found in the subjects of folklore, natural history, and traditional forms of southern hunting. His PhD from the University of North Carolina is in history, and he has edited an anthology of North Carolina nature writers and compiled a history of a vast hunt club on Hilton Head Island that survived until vacation development became the chief industry of the island and sport hunting was pushed elsewhere. He's probably thought longer and deeper about southern hunting than almost anyone.

Richard grew up in once-rural Gaston County, North Carolina, the descendant of early settlers. His family still owns land there, so it's not a surprise that his interest in hunting and local hunting culture would find object in one of the remaining traditional hunts. He became involved in the hunt when David Helms, the beloved, eighty-year-old maintenance man at his school, invited the headmaster to come out one Friday night and join the old hunt.

When Richard first told me of his latest hunting research what came to mind was what one usually thinks of as a typical fox hunt, what some call "tally-ho hunting." But Richard wasn't compiling a study of wealthy people in red coats and funny helmets blowing horns and riding horses as packs of hounds take off through the gentrified countryside. He was interested in groups of old Gaston County farmers who sit around the fire, tell stories, and listen as their hounds range through the woods. "The dogs hardly ever catch anything," Richard told me when I talked with him about accompanying him on the hilltop hunt. "But the old men still hunt once or twice a week, and I've taken to sitting with them and listening, taking notes."

Richard says the old men know their dogs by their individual voices. When I witnessed the hunt would they yell, "There goes Old Blue" as the pack of hounds circled in the distance. Richard says the men don't use guns. In the old days when this activity was still multigenerational, Richard says some of the young men would actually get out and run with the dogs like a hunting practice right out of the late Paleolithic.

Besides Richard's interest, much of what I know about the larger cultural context of hilltop fox chasing comes from Thad Sitton's account of the vanishing activity in *Gray Ghosts and Red Rangers*, his 2010 study of what is now more often referred to as a "lost folkway" than a living tradition.

All indications are that this type of hunting with hounds persisted everywhere throughout the rural South from its settlement until about 1980. When the hunting began, dogs often chased deer, fox, whatever, and then by 1980 there wasn't much of any large game to hunt except foxes. Most of the large wild mammals and obvious game birds had been depleted or had vanished entirely—deer, turkey, ducks, geese, bear. The foxes, both the hybridized red and the solely native gray, survived in the farm country that made up much of the South until about forty years ago, and the farmers turned their hounds out to chase them. There were advantages: the hunting kept down the fox population (fewer chickens lost to predation), but most of all, the neighborhood fox hunts created community. Now this type of fox hunting has become a rare and endangered experience, perfect territory for Richard Rankin to bring his history training to bear.

So why is this hilltop fox hunting so rare today, and why am I interested in it in a book about coyotes coming into the South? The return of deer to much of the South in the 1960s and 1970s diverted most people's attention to the type of hunting we're more familiar with. Men left the comfort of the circle around the fire, bought high-powered rifles and high-tech bows, and climbed alone into tree stands. They banded together and leased tracts of land for expansive hunt clubs and sold memberships granting the privilege to hunt there. Even the dogs became confused. At the few remaining hilltop hunts when the men set the hounds loose, they were just as likely to pick up the scent of a deer (now numerous) as that of a fox.

Then there were property rights issues as well. As the rural South became the suburban, bedroom-community South, rural people often posted their land, and fewer people enjoyed the idea of a pack of hounds running all night through their one-acre yard on the edge of the country in pursuit of wild game. It became harder and harder to find large tracts of rural land. Paved, straight roads bisected the old farm country, and the farmers lost their dogs to high-speed modern traffic.

And so the old hilltop hunting culture vanished in most places, but the idea persisted in a rudimentary form. Compounds of two hundred to a thousand acres were fenced in some places, and a new generation of sportsmen took their fox hunting "inside," running expensive pedigree hounds after fenced foxes, and more and more often—enter my interests—imported coyotes in the enclosed field trials. Folkway became mostly sport. Tradition became leisure activity. Local culture was lost and left to historians like Richard to document. Dog food companies even sponsored these competitions.

"What should I bring?" I'd asked Richard earlier on the phone.

"A six-pack of diet Mountain Dew and a can of peanuts," he'd said.

As I followed Richard through the rural southern countryside I began to inventory the poems I could remember that might shed some light on what I was about to experience. In his poem "Listening to Fox Hounds," James Dickey recalls experiences he had in the mountains of north Georgia as a boy. In it the speaker takes his place in a circle of men in the woods watching for when "the first tone of a dog on a scent" lights up one of the listening faces.

After talking with Richard about Wade Ward's farm I also listened to something lighter than the James Dickey poem, a traditional blue-grass song, "Like a Fox on the Run"—"She walks through the corn leadin' down to the river / Her hair shone like gold in the hot mornin' sun / She took all the love that a poor boy could give her / And left me to die like a fox on the run / Like a fox, like a fox, like a fox on the run." Maybe the ole boy who wrote that song had been out with his uncles and neighbors on a fox hunt and found the inspiration for his lyrics sitting around their fire, listening to their stories of love and loss, the fox and the hounds running in the distance. So many of the lyrics of good bluegrass songs came straight out of that vanishing rural culture. Maybe today the song needed to talk about foxes and coyotes on the run.

Where will future southern poets and songwriters find their lyrics of wildness and love and loss now that the farms and dairies are vanishing and the suburbs are filling in the spaces between the cities? It's hard to imagine writing a song about chasing a coyote inside a fenced enclosure and Old Blue's owner getting points in a trial every time the dog passes a judging stand draped with banners for brands of dog food.

These lyric reflections on rural southern hunting led me in many directions, but did little to clarify coyotes in my mind. As I drove I thought about confusion, speculation, and scientific research about how coyotes actually reached the Atlantic Ocean. There's little doubt that the coyote's presence here has a great deal to do with the very hilltop hunting I'd be witnessing, and particularly those fox pens. However they got here, they are successful by anyone's measure. There's little doubt that the medium-sized predator has now colonized all available forested and agricultural habitats in North America. They are increasingly sighted even in East Coast urban and suburban areas, Boston, Washington, and Atlanta. In 1999 a young coyote was caught in Manhattan's Central Park; today coyotes are regulars in the park and all the boroughs of the city. Like Pale Male, the famous Central Park red-tail hawk, the city coyotes even have names. His admirers named the 1999 Central Park coyote Otis, and in 2006 a coyote named Hal was captured but died just before he was to be released on private land just outside Manhattan. In the summer of 2007 an unnamed coyote ambled into a Quizno's in downtown Chicago and sat in the store's beverage cooler for almost an hour until animal control officers finally captured and removed the loiterer. In 2015 a family outside Atlanta returned home and found a coyote sitting on the kitchen counter next to the toaster.

In the southeastern cities, coyotes are now so common that they are often the subjects of town hall meetings, and neighborhoods hire their own private trappers when they're not happy with their local government's response to sightings and missing pets. By 2007 a private trapper had caught nine coyotes near the Atlanta Country Club, and trappers have even started advertising on local community "e-alert" networks for professional coyote removal.

In 1995 Gerry Parker published *The Eastern Coyote*, as yet still the only full book-length study of coyote's colonization of eastern North America. Parker, a Canadian biologist and researcher (now retired), had been a hunter and occasional trapper as well, and his book is divided into fourteen chapters and an epilogue. Early in his study Parker notes the "impressive . . . phenomenon of coyote range extension" while also offering what seems an even-handed examination of coyote ecology, the place of predators in the eastern landscapes, and possible realistic strategies for their future management. There's even a rhymed poem by Parker at the volume's end that shows his sympathy and admiration for coyotes and offers a note of warning for those predator haters full of simple misunderstanding: "So take time to reflect before casting that stone / And rushing to lay the blame / For the conflict is old and fears run deep / And it's not yet the end of the game."

By the time of Parker's book's publication "the game" was pretty far along though, even in the South. Scientists speak of this ecological movement east as an occupation, a colonization, a range extension, a dispersion, a proliferation, and very often an invasion, as if coyotes were pushing into the region like Normans crossing the English Channel from France in 1066.

Researchers might have trouble agreeing on what to call the impressive range extension, but few would argue with Parker calling it "a success story, one of ecological and behavioral flexibility, which has seen the coyote capitalize on the smallest of opportunities to successfully multiply and move on to occupy new territories."

Gerry Parker was one of the first to popularize the idea that the occupation of the east utilized two "fronts," one northern, which began a hundred years earlier, skirting the Great Lakes and extending into northern New England by the 1920s and veering down later into New York and Pennsylvania. The southern front of colonization followed through Texas and Arkansas, and it crossed the Mississippi River in the late 1960s. The charts illustrating these migrations of coyotes cast look like something you'd see in a Civil War encyclopedia with big arrows sweeping forces into battle.

Parker introduced me to the idea that it's not entirely accurate to imagine the southern coyotes behind our house as simply migrating western creatures colonizing, as if they had walked from great distances to populate our backyards with a wild, clever canine carnivore again. The dates sprinkled over the battle map—1940, 1960, 1970—hint at a much more complex ecological battle line. The scattered dates are confirmed releases ("liberations," as Parker calls them) for coyotes in the South. These animals arrived as captives from the West and then either escaped or were released, most likely, as prey to train trailing dogs. As fox hunter Ben Hardaway says near the end of his autobiography *Never Outfoxed*, "There may be some question in the minds of the State Fish and Game biologists as to how the coyote crossed the Mississippi River in the eastern migration, but there is no question in my mind—he crossed in a crate on the back of a pickup driven by a Georgia foxhunter."

If wild coyotes came into our country through releases, what they have achieved is maybe even more stunning. Yes, they've migrated in a moving "front," a southern wave sweeping in from the West over the past fifty years after first crossing the Mississippi on our bridges and colonizing Mississippi, Georgia, Tennessee, South Carolina, and North Carolina, but these migrating pioneers also met others along the way, coyotes escaped from fox pens, liberated into our midst, to become small cells of wild canine insurgents. The descendants of these coyotes found ways to live close by us over the last few decades without many of us even noticing, until their numbers grew. Now that we have noticed, hate them or not, they have enlivened our suburban deserts of fescue, house cats, poodles, and crepe myrtle with mystery and unpredictability. And so, what to do with them now that these southern coyotes find themselves free and wild in a distant foreign land? How do we all make the best of it?

One method for making the best of it is to honor the old ways, so, near dark, Richard finally called to say he was close and we'd leave my truck at a McDonald's outside Kings Mountain. I soon loaded into his pickup with my sack of snacks. When I opened the truck's door Richard looked more the part of country gentleman than I did. He wore a white canvas hat and muck boots, and he pointed out the chair he'd brought to sit in—a straight-backed cane-seated wooden chair, which was much more traditional than my $3.99 green Wal-Mart special. I could tell Richard was excited about what I would experience that evening because he launched right in: "You'll love Wade. He looks like a hilltop hunter is supposed to look," he said.

As we drove we talked about the differences between "hunting outside," like we'd see that night, and "hunting inside." We both agreed that from our points of view there was a diminishment of something authentic once you put up a fence and run dogs after captive foxes and coyotes and give prizes out. I paraphrased the last paragraph of Thad Sitton's *Gray Ghosts and Red Rangers*, how the old-time hilltop fox hunt asserts the persistence of wilderness in the landscape, and how during the chase "men are beasts as well as men."

Then in the presence of a friend I expressed disgust for the practice of these fox pens, something the level-headed anthropologist Thad Sitton never does, but I admitted that the idea of old-time, hilltop hunting seemed romantic to me and even exciting. I have no issue with this old form of rural hunting where the quarry has a good chance of getting away alive, and if the folk song has any truth to it, the foxes and coyotes might actually enjoy eluding the dogs on a good chase.

In contrast, there is little redeemable about the fox pen industry. Throw thirty or forty foxes into a big cage together—even if it is a thousand-acre cage—and the result will be disease, depredation, and destruction. How could something as pastoral as old-time hilltop hunting turn so bad and become fox penning? Fox pens may be as bad as old-time prison incarceration. Or old state mental hospitals. They may be just as crazy making. They may be as full of the human destructive mind as anything we've created.

"They talk about 'going in the pen,' and something must be lost," Richard said. "It used to be they would hilltop hunt two times a week. It must have been very important to them."

We left the four-lane and turned down one rural road after another, zagging deeper into real country, not simple suburban edges bleeding into tree lots. We even passed what Richard called "a brush arbor."

"These were the first churches in this area," he explained. He said originally some rural congregations constructed shelters for the services out of brush, and the temporary structures still survive in some deeply rural places, "though now they build them out of two-by-fours and plywood. This is deep country. The presence of this arbor proves it."

We finally turned onto gravel and left the paved secondary road behind. "This is Wade's driveway," Richard said with a mounting sense of excitement. A long gravel one-track curved into the hardwoods along both sides. There were little garden plots, and a dozen rabbits hopped into the weeds as we passed.

The cell phone rang, bringing us back to the twenty-first century, and Richard looked at the number. "That's Wade," he said. "Hey, Wade, we're on your road."

There was still a little light in the west but it was closing in on dead dark. In the summer in the South this is the magic time when the heat finally collapses and storms build on the horizon. We didn't have much heat that evening, but the sky threatened a storm anyway. I hoped it would hold off until after the hunt.

Soon we passed Wade's house—a brick one-story ranch in the woods—and just past that, his dog yard where fifteen hounds were chained to blue plastic barrels. They bayed as we drove by. Wade's pickup waited at a spot near one of his old barns. He had a dog cage in the back of the truck and, to my surprise, it contained not a hunting hound, but a big, friendly German shepherd.

Wade stepped out when we pulled up, dressed in worn blue work shirt and pants and an old dirty trucker hat. He let the dog loose and then shook my hand. He was missing three fingers on his right hand, but his grip was firm, even though it came from only his index finger and a thumb.

I liked Wade right away. He reminded me of my uncles in eastern North Carolina I'd been around as a child. They were farmers and had the same easy way about them as Wade had—the same smile and rugged exterior, scraped and scarred by contact with the rural world around them. Almost all of them were missing fingers too.

Wade saw me looking at the big wood stove and the woodpile the road circled around, and he spoke for the first time. He spoke like he had a mouth full of knuckle-sized gravel, not like he had a speech impediment, just an accent heavy enough to grind any sentence into slurry. "That's the tipi where the bullshitting takes place in the wintertime," he drawled.

Wade didn't want to stand around. Silence and stillness seemed to make him nervous, so we walked up an intersecting gravel road along the edge of another of his fields, this one a little bigger than the garden plots we'd seen driving in, but had not been planted yet, and stubble covered the ground. Richard asked about the crops, and Wade explained how he'd planted wheat the year before and that he'd get around to planting soon, but wasn't sure with what yet. He said he's a full-time farmer now after thirty years as part-time farmer and full-time heavy equipment operator. "I used to work all day and come home and drive the tractor all night. I thought it would get easier once I retired. I was wrong."

I scratched Wade's German shepherd behind the ears, and Wade said, "You won't be able to touch the others like that. They'll let me handle them, but nobody else."

"How many dogs will you run tonight?" I asked.

"I'll cast thirteen," Wade said. I'd never heard that verb used in quite that way before. It made sense once I thought about it. For an oldtime hunter like Wade, dogs are the instrument of the hunt, not the hunt itself, something to cast, like a net or dice or scratch to feed the chickens.

By the time we got back to the tipi, two other pickups had pulled up and several of Wade's friends were waiting in folding chairs: John Huffsteter and a man by the name of Forrest. Richard had told me John might be there and that he and his late father were legend among the local hunters. They'd kept lots of dogs and hunted for generations.

Unlike Wade, they were deeply connected into the regionwide world of formal foxhound trials and networks of hunt clubs where John deer hunted. I unfolded my cheap green camp chair and settled in next to John. Richard pulled his straight-back wooden chair out of his truck bed and took a spot between Forrest and Wade.

For the next thirty minutes, until it was really dark, I talked with John Huffsteter. When I asked, he told me how he'd seen the first coyote at his place (about ten miles away from Wade's farm) fifteen years earlier.

You can tell a great deal about someone's relationship to *Canis latrans* by the way they pronounce its common name. Many, like John Huffsteter, say "ky-yoat," snuffing silent the ultimate e, and others (and I am among them) say "ky-oat-tee," lingering on the long e and giving the vowel prominence. There are linguistic purists who say that since it's a Spanish word, we should pronounce it ko(long o) yo(long o) ta (long a).

"I was sitting on my porch," John continued, "and saw what I thought was two German shepherds chasing a deer in the pasture. I had my pistol and I shot one. I soon found I'd shot my first ky-yoat."

John told me, as had others, that he thought the insurance companies had introduced the coyotes into the South to control the deer. He could have been baiting me. He had to know the coming of the coyote to this landscape was more complex than rumor. I decided it wasn't worth arguing the point, and so I just continued to listen. I liked John, though he was more worldly and practiced than Wade was. You could see the difference in the two of them in their pickup trucks if nothing else. Wade's old truck looked like it was made for tooling around the farm. John's was newer and made for hauling trailers, but also for driving miles in comfort. Mostly it was the way they told stories that was different, though. John told stories as if he'd told them many times before, and I guess he had, with probably thousands of hours sitting around waiting for a hunt, or listening to a hunt in the distance, or sitting around in some faraway deer camp with a half-dozen men in from a day in a tree stand. Some of John's stories intrigued me. He reminded me how gray foxes can climb trees and red foxes can't. He told of turning up a gray fox and a set of pups in an old sawmill's slab pile, and then turning up the slabs nearby and catching the male as well. He speculated on how gray foxes avoid the mange that ravages red foxes and coyotes because they often den in those old slab piles at sawmills. "It could be something about the pine resin," he said. "That's all I can figure."

When Wade heard us talking about coyotes he stood up and wandered out in front and added a couple of stories of his own. He said dogs don't generally like chasing coyotes. "They're a little scared of them. Sometimes the coyotes will get right out and run along with them like they're trailing something too." He said he'd been mowing a field a time or two and had seen coyotes come out of the trees to chase the mice that had been scared up, and he described one winter hunt on the farm when the dogs had cornered a coyote on an island in the frozen pond. "They didn't want to go over there after it," he said. "I had to clap my hands before they'd go."

John told a few more stories, and then he turned quiet, almost reverent. "You know, we can talk about things like this forever and never get to the truth of it."

I wondered about this truth John was concerned with. Was I trying to get to the truth about coyotes, or was I just interested in hearing some stories? Did he mean that no matter how many stories you tell you can never get to the bottom of the natural history of wild animals like coyotes, or that there is always some mystery to the way wild animals act, or that there is some truth that is always elusive when people start telling stories about things in nature? Then again, he might have just been messing with me.

A few minutes later Wade announced it was time to load up, and I folded my chair and Wade put his dog in the cage in the truck bed again. Forrest climbed in the cab of Wade's truck, and they drove off toward the dog yard. John put his tailgate down, and Richard and I sat on it, cheek and jowl with John's four caged dogs. They licked my fingers through the wire.

We rode a few hundred yards like this, bouncing on the tailgate, with a Chuck-will's-widow calling in the dark farm field to our right. All the dogs howled and called as Wade backed his truck in, got his pet dog out, and started loading the hunting hounds, one by one. He packed them in the cage where they shifted back and forth and waited. The hounds to be left behind tethered to their blue barrels howled, barked, whined, sometimes eight or ten barks in a row. All through it, unseen in the dark, Wade instructed his friends as to which dogs he wanted in the cages on the back of the pickup. In the distance the Chuck-will's-widow kept up its three-note chorus. As we watched the men load these dogs I thought of my own overweight beagle Murphy back home on the couch. Should I have brought him along? Should I have turned him loose like Woodrow or Dickey's foxhounds to run in the old ways with the pack through the bottom land?

Soon we were moving again, John following Wade up to the hilltop where they would let the dogs loose. We left the gravel road and crossed a ditch, and the truck bounced along a tree line with the paved road we'd come in on beyond that, our feet brushing the tops of broom straw in the fields, the dark outline of the hilltop ahead of us, another Chuck-will's-widow calling to the first in the distance behind us.

The two trucks circled and Wade and John climbed out. We hopped off the tailgate, and with no ceremony, Wade and John tripped the latches on the cages. The sixteen hounds tumbled out into the night where they began to sniff around on the unmowed hilltop. The moment was so silent compared to the loading of the dogs. Nobody said anything, and I watched as most of the hounds formed up in a pack and took off down the slope toward a tree line barely visible in the distance and darkness. A very old dog and a young dog—both John's—lagged behind, as if they preferred the predictable company of men on the hill to the chase heating up in the distance.

While it was still light enough to see just a little, I asked Wade about the landscape, and he explained how Buffalo Creek was behind us. I knew the creek as part of the Broad River drainage where I lived, and I'd even paddled by the mouth of it once on a float trip. That gave me a real comfort, the idea that this hunt was happening in my watershed and not in some distant place. Then Wade told me names of other landmarks on the farm: "There's the Hill Place, the Whipper Place, the Pines, the Bluff on Buffalo, the 'Simmon Tree, the Forks of the Creek," Wade said, pointing in various directions at familiar places lost in the deepening dark.

Another pickup pulled up, and out slid a younger man, who introduced himself as Wade's nephew. Richard pulled out his chair, sat down, and began a prolonged conversation with the new arrival, and I wandered off to listen to Wade, Forrest, and John tracking the distant dogs.

"They got a run goin' over by the junkyard."

"When they runnin' a fox they'll be a steady voice. A coyote will be like that too."

"This time of year you got young fox and young coyotes."

"They're right there. Hear 'em?"

"They'll be up at Highway 150."

"They're comin' this way."

Wade looked at me and said, "Cup your ears and you can hear the dogs better." I put my hands up around my ears and he was right, the whole night world came sharply into focus. The one distant cacophony of the pack broke apart into the individual voices. I even heard and distinguished other night sounds besides the loud-mounted Chuck-will's-widows.

"They coming this way."

"Come on, Virginia."

"Coming out far down there some of 'em are coming out to the left."

"Lead dog is ole Jake. They'll get through them fences, get through 'em in a minute."

"What are their names?" I asked Wade as we listened.

"Oh you know, regular dog names, Spot, Junior, Jake, Queen, Blackjack, Bill, Jeff, Becky, Tina, and three dogs called Virginia."

"Could be a young gray fox up against the highway," John said. I was impressed with how well they knew the topography. It was all black night to me. These men were able to follow the dogs anywhere they went, any turn they made. The dogs were navigating to the scents on the wind, and the old men were tracking them like radar stations with their extended ears as the dogs rounded and romped past fencerows, ditches, runnels, gullies, thorn-banks, seeps, and springs.

"They running something young," Wade said.

"Coming back up," John answered.

"Really hear 'em now."

"Are they following a scent?" I asked.

"Fox dogs don't run like beagles. A beagle'll run a track but a fox dog will run the wind," John explained.

"What's different about the way a coyote runs and how a fox runs?"

"A coyote will run in a circle just like a fox, and then it might just take off and run in a straight line all the way to Spartanburg," Wade said.

The excitement built as the hounds turned and headed back across the field. We couldn't see them, but the sound grew louder and louder as they passed below us in the dark and headed off into the distance.

I wanted to imagine that they were chasing a wily coyote who somehow enjoyed eluding this pack of dogs on his tail. That he too knew the voices of the familiar foe—the Virginias, Jake, Jenny in hot pursuit. And that he knew every way of throwing the hounds off and leading them where only he knew to hide and slip and double back.

"Do you ever lose one?" I asked. "A hound, I mean."

John got quiet for moment before he answered.

"It's just like a run of bad luck," he said. "It comes in threes. They'll be one dog hit by a car, then a week later another, then another. Then it might be a year. It's more now than it used to be."

"Let's load up. Time to go back to the tipi," Wade said.

I dropped my hands from around my ears. Wade saw me looking at the time on my phone and said, "Daylight, they'll all come in."

As the dogs grew closer Richard walked up to listen. "I think we'll be out of here in an hour."

John glanced over at me and said, "Boys, this the way huntin' is. Three or four in the morning is when you hear something."

Forrest saw me looking at the time too, nodded toward John: "Last week he stayed all night and got all his dogs back in."

"Do you sleep when they stay out all night?" I asked.

"Hell no," Wade said. "I get right there on the ground. It is just like laying in the bed. Laying on the ground you can hear them better than standing up."

"Jake's going across the knob," John added.

"You must have your hearing aid in," Wade said.

At the end of *Woodrow's Trumpet* the modern suburban world has finally closed in and Woodrow goes on one last hunt. He casts his hounds and listens as they follow not the scent trail left by wild animals but a survey path left by crews laying out subdivisions, and instead of coming upon a raccoon or a fox they corner and kill a domestic cat instead. "The wilderness is gone from here," he thinks as he approaches his confused dogs. He blows one last time on his hunting horn and the wilderness dies.

As I drove back to Spartanburg I chased two opposing ideas for sixty miles. The first is that hilltop fox and coyote hunting like it's practiced in the rural country north of Kings Mountain is a tradition as instructive about country life as molasses making or seed saving, and it needs to survive. This idea is the one suggested by Dickey's poem and McLaurin's novel, and it goes back to Faulkner—"The Bear" and "Delta Autumn" come to mind. In the first story a young Isaac McCaslin witnesses the Mississippi wilderness—"tall and endless"—through the eyes of the old hunters like Sam Fathers and Major de Spain, but he also sees "man's puny gnawing at the immemorial flank." In "Delta Autumn," old Uncle Ike travels in a car to the last hunting camp deep in the Delta and finds solace thinking about how he and the wilderness have about the same life left and that he will not outlive it.

The second idea is that this type of hunting, and by extension the old ways such as McLaurin, Dickey, and Faulkner write about, have outrun their time, and when this generation passes the young folks probably shouldn't and won't continue them. Thinking this way, hunting with dogs is an anachronism evolved out of values and filling needs that no longer exist. Over time the working breeds themselves may not exist except mostly as pets, like the sweet-natured German shepherd in the back of Wade's truck.

What is sad about the second line of thinking is that all that will remain of "the old ways" when hilltop hunting vanishes is the pen running. I'd asked Wade about this earlier in the evening—whether even the pens would survive—and he'd thought for a minute and said they probably wouldn't. Even the pen owners in his area were getting up in years, and the operations were expensive to maintain, and new people moving in don't like it when they find out what's going on behind the high fence.

One thing was sure though, if they can beat the mange and heartworms, coyotes are here to stay. On summer nights in the future the Chuck-will's-widow will still call, and the coyotes will come out to hunt and howl, whether Wade's or John's hounds are there to chase them or not.

Coyote Hugger

I believe children can be helped to hear the many voices
about them. Take time to listen and talk and [hear] the voices
of the earth and what they mean.—Rachel Carson

A few months later I drove to Aiken, South Carolina, to
meet Scooter, maybe the only captive coyote legally maintained in
the state for educational purposes. On the day we met, Scooter the
coyote waited in his large plastic kennel, hidden under a blue denim
cover. The kennel was posted with signs that said, "DO NOT TOUCH"
on the three visible sides. There were four other crates, green plastic
ones like you'd store sweaters in for winter, stacked alongside the kennel. Two of the crates still sat on the red dolly Sean Poppy, Scooter's
keeper, used to roll them inside Millbrook Baptist preschool for the
summer nature program. There were also two smaller kennels with a
camo and a blue cloth cover side-by-side on the makeshift stage. The
stacked containers made the stage look like the set for a magic show
or a moving sale.

Many adults, Sean said, just don't get why anyone would keep a live
coyote. Why keep a vermin? Best to just shoot it, they say. When Sean
found Scooter as an orphan puppy "scooting" across the highway—
ant-bit, malnourished, dehydrated—even a few of his colleagues at the
lab said, "Oh, that's great, raising a coyote puppy. He'll turn on you
when he's a year old." It didn't happen. Scooter was now two and a
half, and Sean said he's getting nicer to work with as he gets older, not
harder. "Now he'll get on his back and let me rub his belly."

It was not a stage, actually. Sean had merely defined an area at the front of the elementary school classroom by his considerable presence and hidden surprises. The chairs and desks before him were numerous and small enough to fit in a Hobbit house, but the children filed in and sat on the floor instead. Despite the shushing and threats to pull them out by the two stern teachers, the children made comments as they filed into the classroom. The teachers were not amused. "Mr. Poppy will tell you where to sit," one of the women said when the children looked unsure how close to approach.

"I don't like snakes. Do you have snakes?" one little girl asked, taking a back row seat on the floor.

Until the little girl spoke I'd forgotten how much fear defines the boundaries of many of our interactions with wildlife. Of course the fear of snakes is atavistic in many humans, especially contemporary humans who are bombarded by media images of dangerous animals—like the pythons invading the Everglades and great white sharks at the beach. It's a miracle some little girl in a Baptist preschool doesn't just stand up and run screaming from the room.

"You came to Chukker Creek Elementary once. You brought a coyote," another little boy said, and pushed forward.

On the top green crate the flaps were open, and inside I could see various cloth bags, some moving a little, and Solo deli cups and Sterilite ShowOffs containers ready to be opened and reveal their secret contents to the audience. It looked like little could fluster Sean. He'd seen most of this before. For sixteen years he's worked for the Savannah River Ecology Lab Outreach Program where he's now the coordinator. He does programs like this three hundred times a year, often several times a day. He stood meditatively in front of the arriving children. Of medium height and compact, he wore his jet black hair pulled back in a ponytail. The logo of the blue SREL polo shirt he wore is an embroidered spotted salamander, the state amphibian of South Carolina. Sean has the perfect temperament for these programs—calm, attentive, but steady. His patience, as he'd explained to me earlier, came in handy raising a coyote.

Even though he's named Scooter, Sean knows he's a wild coyote. "Yes, he's wild. He gets possessive of things and has a totally different look in his eyes than a dog. I've gotten used to that." Sean always reminds everyone, all the time, how Scooter's not a pet, how it's good to have a practiced routine for handling a wild canine. "I write my own protocols. I wear gloves even when I walk him on the leash. We've had several sessions of roughhousing. He play-bites. He tests me. I've had to set him straight, pin him down so he couldn't move." Despite the protocol, Sean's been through four sets of welding gloves. Raising a wild dog means you're going to get bitten and scratched. "I lost a lot of blood."

Scooter's survival is a testament to Sean's devotion to him. He's put his own resources, not those of the program, into Scooter's care and housing. But there is more. Sean has built a respectful, strong relationship with this creature who would have been dead had he not been rescued from beside a South Carolina road as a puppy.

As I watched Sean prepare his nature show I thought of precedents for this story—of course there is Marjorie Kennan Rawling's *The Yearling*, the 1938 novel where sometime in backcountry Florida in the nineteenth century young Jody Baxter wants a pet but his mother reminds him they barely have enough food to feed themselves. In a complex plot twist that involves a bear, a rattlesnake, and the liver of a shot doe, Jody finds a fawn that he adopts and names Flag. They are together all the time. As Flag grows from fawn to adult, he eats the Baxters' corn and endangers their very survival. As you would guess, this story of wild meets domestic in *The Yearling* does not end well. Jody is forced to shoot Flag and runs away. Jody does finally return home, but his innocence is lost forever.

In a more contemporary tale, Barry Lopez explains in the epilogue to *Of Wolves and Men* how he raised two hybrid coyote–red wolf pups,

Prairie and River, in a pen behind his house for a few years. A wildlife park, likely part of a breeding effort in the early 1970s in Oregon to reintroduce red wolves to the South, abandoned the two puppies. This adoption effort did not end well either, as Prairie and River escaped after someone left their gate open. River was shot and Prairie bolted for the woods.

From raising these wild animals Lopez learns much in their presence, but he concludes, "If we are going to learn more about animals—real knowledge, not more facts—we are going to have get out into the woods. We are going to have to pay more attention to free-ranging as opposed to penned animals, which will require an unfamiliar patience." Lopez's book was written near the end of the twentieth century, maybe one of bloodiest for wildlife ever. Lopez believed then that as the twentieth century came to a close "an understanding of animals different from the one that has guided us for the past 300 years" must emerge. About what he had learned raising a wild red wolf named River, Lopez said, "I learned from River I was a human being and that he was a wolf and that we were different. I valued him as a creature, but he did not have to be what I imagined he was."

Scooter doesn't stay outside at night like Prairie, River, or Flag. He spends his nights in a ten-by-fifteen-foot kennel in the Poppy family garage. Sean carries him there from his daytime enclosure. The kennel has indoor plumbing and a big bathtub full of clumping cat litter. Sean gave Scooter a comfortable floppy dog bed, but the coyote ate it. He likes to sleep on the concrete, always on top of an old blue flannel shirt. There are chew toys scattered throughout the kennel—a section of plastic drainpipe, a bone, and his favorite, a purple plastic Kong. Sean turns on a fan that runs all night to drone out the barking dogs outside that make the coyote nervous. I remembered as I was looking at Scooter's toys that my brother-in-law's neighbor had told a story about catching a coyote on camera gnawing the tops off his in-ground sprinkler system and then playing with the pieces. Sounds believable.

Looking at the nighttime pen, I asked Sean about Scooter's health. Sean's sister's a veterinarian, so he gets a break on the care. "She had to run three different drugs through him to get rid of all the parasites. He made it through the first night and my sister said, 'he's got a chance.'" The day before I met him Scooter had had his yearly shots and had passed this year's vector-borne disease test. "The summer before he got some parasites, though," Sean explained. "He eats anything he can find. He digs up shrews. He seems to like to hear them squeak. I brought him persimmons when he was little and he'll also eat blueberries. He was eating a few weeds this morning."

Since Sean found Scooter this "education animal" has worked shifts like this one at the preschool for his keep, a daily cup of dog kibble and a few raw deer tenderloin treats Sean cuts from local roadkill. Scooter sat in the dark while Sean began the program. Scooter's always the last performer in the show. "The kids love him because he's a mammal," Sean had told me earlier. Scooter seemed comfortable sitting quietly and waiting. "When he's in a program he sits quiet in the crate. When I take him out I hold him."

"At the ecology lab we learn everything you can about the outdoors," Sean finally began, "plants, animals, soils. I like animals, and I hope you do too. But don't try to handle a wild animal." Sean reached in the open green crate and picked up a small plastic bowl with a lid, and a little water sloshed around as he unsnapped the top. "I'll get out a few animals." This was Sean's standard program for kids, a modulated survey of the animal kingdom with interesting living props. Sean starts in the middle of the epic story of life, from bacteria to mammals. He starts with a frog.

The frog came out of his plastic cup, and Sean held him by a front leg. "He's very slippery. He can climb up the wall. What sort of frog is this?"

"Tree frog!" about five students intoned.

"Right, a green tree frog. Long hind legs," and Sean extended the long leg out to show them. "As scientists studying tree frogs we just go out and listen," Sean continued and pulled out his old flip phone to play an audio file. "Do you even know what a flip phone is?"

"My grandmother had one," a little girl deadpanned.

Sean played the file and the sound, like someone tooting on a little tin horn, filled the room.

He put the tree frog away and took out a bullfrog.

"Oooooh!" said the group in unison.

The bullfrog's big long legs dangled from Sean's hand. "Look at those front feet. Look at those little hands."

"Could he swallow a baby's arm? Could he if he wanted to?" the vocal boy asked from the back row.

Sean seemed a little perplexed by this question. "Well, I think that would be a little too much," he finally said and moved on to the next animal from another container.

Sean pulled out a salamander, the same one that was on the logo on his shirt. "This is a spotted salamander. Shaped like a lizard but it's not. Look at his head. It's shaped like a little door wedge. When we want to study these, we have to go out on a rainy night. We can catch these, and they can tell us the health of the environment."

The salamander sat calmly in his palm. "The natural oil from my hand can harm his sensitive skin. I won't hold him too long." Then Sean opened another plastic box and pulled out a gregarious box turtle.

"Turtle! Turtle!" the crowd chanted.

Sean pointed out its red eyes. "It's a male."

And then Sean followed the box turtle with a big snapping turtle from its own personal green crate.

"Wow!" one child said and moved back a little.

The snapper craned out his long neck and made a huffing sound.

"He's mad!" one of the girls screamed.

"We're one of his predators. He's afraid, so he's breathing like Darth Vader," Sean joked.

Sean put the snapping turtle back in his box and said what the children had really been waiting to hear, "Now we're gonna look at a few snakes."

"Ahhhhhh!" screamed the little girl who had already reported her fear.

"My daddy took us four-wheeling and we saw a big king snake," the vocal boy on the back row added in excitement.

Sean uncoiled a two-foot scarlet king snake. "What's that rhyme?"

"Red on yellow. Hurt a fellow. Red on black. Friend of Jack," another boy proudly reported.

"Yes, that's right. And what is this one?"

"Red on black."

"So we know it's a friend of Jack."

"Does he bite?" the little girl with the snake fear asked.

"He has to bite to live," another girl huffed with some exasperation.

The star of the snake show was a gray rat snake Sean pulled out next, maybe five feet long.

"I caught this snake crossing the road," Sean said. "He had already been hit by a car, and then when I stopped, I saw two more cars run over him. I thought he would be dead and so I'd take him back to the lab to be used as a specimen. Somehow he survived. Most of the damage was to this section." (He points to the lower third of the snake's body.) "We're lucky they didn't hit his head. He can't aim well. He's going to be an education animal the rest of his life. Now he's our rat snake."

After the snakes came the alligators, first a yearling, maybe ten inches long, and then a longer two-year-old, maybe two feet. Sean held the bigger alligator up for everyone to see how long it was.

"Does it do the death roll?" the vocal boy asked. "If he bites you and starts to do the death roll, you can't get loose."

"He's been handled since he was a baby," Sean said. "We don't have to worry about the death roll."

"Do you have True TV?" the boy continued. "On there this guy kissed a fish and it just snapped at him."

"I don't have cable," Sean said, moving quickly on.

I laughed to myself. Reality TV is pervasive (and persuasive) now in the minds of these children. The world of real animals in a real classroom merges seamlessly in their consciousness. Almost all have seen *Gator Hunter*, or *Duck Dynasty*, and all unconsciously compared the action of these shows with the animal presences before them. There isn't a great deal of what Aldo Leopold called an "ecological consciousness" in these TV shows, the idea that we humans have a responsibility for the health and preservation of the land and all its parts. These shows are mostly anthropocentric in theme, and often pitched as if there is no ethical dilemma or responsibility to lethally hunting and trapping wildlife for pleasure. They interact with a world that seems to still be a frontier, open to our human exploits and conquests. Twenty years ago there were folks like Sean Poppy on TV pitching *Wild Kingdom* and *The Crocodile Hunter*. Today the stars are primarily the hook-and-bullet crowd, and the animals are just as likely to end up dead or in a cook pot as in a cloth sack.

It's hard to compete with an edited adventure reality show in the twenty-first century, but Sean held his own if attention is any indicator. Few of the kids turned the channel to stare around the room or shift aimlessly back and forth on their fannies.

"Birds are next because they are similar to alligators," Sean said, and the drama built a little as he reached for one of the birds hidden away behind the cloth covers. "Like reptiles, they lay eggs. They make nests."

Sean removed the camo cover from one of the two bird crates and pulled on a big leather glove, then struggled to get the bird to come out. "He's got to come out. He's got to work."

Finally, Scan pulled the red tailed hawk out, and it sat on his hand like a hunting hawk. There was a tether to keep the bird from flying off, but in spite of this he tried it anyway a couple of times, but couldn't fly far; even so, the children on the front row recoiled a little. After a short flight the hawk settled back on Sean's glove. "He's twenty years old. You know how we know? He was shot from the sky twenty years ago when he was about a year old, and we got him. Probably a farmer shot him. You know they call them chicken hawks. He has to work for his food since then. Two rats a day. That gets expensive."

Then Sean placed the hawk back in its crate and pulled out a great horned owl. "He has big eyes and he can turn his head two hundred and seventy degrees." The owl looked at the crate and Sean couldn't get it to turn. "The crate is a safe place," he explained. "He was hit by a car, the most common way we get owls."

The day before, after Sean showed me Scooter's nighttime quarters, we'd walked out to his daytime enclosure. Scooter the coyote spends the days out in a large D-shaped pen made of six-foot, no-climb horse fence. All the corners are rounded. There are no ninety degree angles. The bottom foot of the fence is curved inward, and the top foot leans inward as well. Sean said coyotes have sensitive feet, and when Scooter was a puppy he'd step on the fence and bound away. It's like having an electric fence without the current, and it discouraged him from digging. "It's worked. I didn't have a book to follow on how to build a coyote fence."

When I looked over at the enclosure I glimpsed a gray presence moving among the pines. "You can go closer," Sean said. I could see Scooter bounding near the rear of the enclosure. I walked up to the fence, and Scooter pounced back, keeping his distance, a gray ghost among the trees, a gray sprite with black highlights, and, as I'd later hear Sean tell the children, a tail that looks like it was "dipped in black paint."

But finally Scooter did come closer. I was close enough to see his sharp snout, his stunning yellow eyes, and his long ears up on alert. His black-tipped tail moved from flowing behind him to tucked between his legs. I was a stranger, not to be trusted, and then Scooter's mammal curiosity would kick in, and he would pause and stand evaluating me.

"It could be the cap. He has this thing about caps. Maybe he thinks we're trying to hide something," Sean said.

Sean keeps the enclosure locked, and the South Carolina Department of Natural Resources permit is posted on the green recycled house door in case someone calls animal control. Being a captive coyote in the suburbs isn't easy. The neighbor's dogs come over and harass him. Sometimes the traffic or other dogs on the road barking sets him on edge. There's a little corrugated roofing shelter for him to go under, but Sean said he seems to like standing in the rain.

"Want to go inside the pen?" Sean asked.

I took off my cap and walked through the door. Sean entered with me. Of course I felt a pang of atavistic fear and childish excitement, but it was quickly overcome by my own curiosity. Scooter's size is not intimidating—he's forty-three pounds and twenty-six inches at the shoulder, about the size of a scrawny German shepherd, but heavier than an average wild coyote. How would Scooter react to my presence in his enclosure? I tucked my cap in my belt and approached him. He moved away like before. I turned my back to him. He padded up closer. He was maybe fifteen feet away when I turned back around. He bounded off into the safety of the pines. When I turned back to face him again and again, he'd bound off into the pines each time. We played this game maybe five or six times, Scooter bounding away, and me turning my back, and him coming closer. Each time when I turned I was a little closer to a wild coyote. There he was—curious about me, wondering (as I was) how close he should really get to this other animal.

I thought about the other time I'd seen a live coyote—in the woods behind our house—and how in control that animal seemed. It saw me and simply padded away at a leisurely pace. I was not a threat or an opportunity for food. There was no other business to transact. Maybe there were pups to feed. No time (or reason) to be sociable.

Distance is very comforting, if it can be kept. Distance allows for all sorts of compromises and adjustments. It's easy to pass laws legalizing night hunting and fox pens when so few are intimate with a new animal like a wild coyote, an animal that summons such deep fears and triggers so many misunderstandings. Imagining there might be some ethical relationship with wild animals only comes through intimate knowledge, as Barry Lopez suggests, like that often possessed (and required) by field biologists, dedicated trappers, ethical hunters, and animal lovers.

Scooter's cousins, the gray wolves, had inched in close to the aboriginal fire for scraps twenty thousand years ago, and look what the choice did for them, *Canis famialiarus*, in all the species' glory. They rolled the evolutionary dice and they won— just like us humans. Their human–canine partnership has been a good one. Dogs keep us company, do some tasks they are programmed for (comfort us in our loneliness; sniff out bombs, drugs, and cancer; pull small loads over snow) and we feed and even coddle them.

If disaster ever strikes the human species and takes out a chunk of our population, the coyote might have the upper hand. Though Scooter was in an enclosure there were cohorts of his ranging all through this human settlement where Sean lives. They know their way around. They keep below the radar mostly. They make a living on our margins, unlike the dogs, who mostly need the comforts we need.

What would become over eons of this new and so far unfamiliar suburban arrangement between wild coyotes and humans in the South? These intelligent creatures are here to stay, and they are interacting with us. Most people want to kill them, to dream they can be eradicated, as westerners once dreamed. Some, like Sean, see coyotes as what they are, parts of a larger, always changing whole, of which we too are only part, and the question is not only how to kill them, but how to live with them, and maybe even how to learn from them, as we go through our own environmental changes.

Would even this experiment in interspecies responsibility and attachment end badly like it did for Marjorie Kennan Rawling's Flag and Barry Lopez's River, or would Scooter live out his natural life as a coyote permitted as an "educational animal" in South Carolina? Lopez focuses heavily in his epilogue on the word "presence," and as I stood with my back to Scooter and then turned to face him I tried as best I could to be there.

"Now we're getting to our last animal," Sean said and stood behind the two green crates. Scooter still waited his turn after the tree frog, the box turtle, the snapping turtle, the two king snakes, the rat snake, the red-tailed hawk, and the great horned owl had warmed up the crowd.

"Coyote!" the kids said almost in unison.

Sean walked over to Scooter's crate and pulled up the flap on the cover and opened the door. "This is not a pet. I hope he'll look really nice to you. If he gets loose he's not going to come after any of you, but if he's cornered that's when we'd see his wildness."

He put on a glove. "I'm going to get him out now and he's scared by loud noises so be quiet. He might bite me if he's scared. When he sees you he'll probably be scared too." Sean reached in and pulled Scooter out. He picked him up and carried him right in front of us to two stacked green crates. The coyote's head drooped, but he looked calm.

"I can feel his heart beat right now. It's racing, but he'll calm down." Scooter sat on the crates with his front paws braced against the edge, his tail tucked under him. "He's not going to like this, but I wanted to show you his tail." Sean reached down and pulled Scooter's long tail out, and we could see it did look like it had been dipped in black paint. "When I'm touching him and I move my hands I think he thinks it's somebody else's hands and he gets nervous. He's very aware of what's going on. Look at his features, his nice eyes and his big ears."

"Is it a girl?" one of the girls asked.

"No this is a boy, a fixed boy."

Sean stood there calmly hugging the coyote to his body, his right arm under the wild dog's belly, and his left arm loosely around his neck. "I'm sure you have heard stories about coyotes. They're here. You don't see them often because they are mostly out at night."

"We hear them," a boy said.

"Yes, you hear them vocalizing. You see how he's shaking?"

Sean kept talking and Scooter looked around, relaxed and observant. "What does he eat?"

"Meat!!!" they said, almost in unison.

"Yes, he eats meat, but he also eats plants. Coyotes are omnivores."

"Berries!"

"Yes, he eats blueberries."

"Yummy!" a little girl said.

"Insects, rodents. They'll work their way up. A lot of people don't like them because they eat baby deer. But he's a scavenger too. Dead animals are easiest for him to catch. He'll just run in a direction of a smell and eat. But they will chase down prey, and some people don't like them because of that."

"So he's your dog?" another girl asked.

"Kinda, but remember, he's not a pet," Sean reminded them.

"Me and my daddy were turkey hunting and a coyote was about as far away as that desk and I leaned a little and I could see a turkey. Stay very still, my daddy said. I'll shoot the coyote and you shoot the turkey," the vocal boy explained in an excited voice.

"So you both were hunting for the same animal," Sean said, smiling.

I was impressed with how Sean handled this. In my mind I'd thought, "So maybe your daddy should let the coyote do what it does. That's real. That's nature. Let him hunt the damn turkey. Marvel at his ability to stalk and kill without Cabelas. Learn some manners. Step down. Take a backseat to a real hunter. The coyote needs it as much, if not more, than you or your daddy does. He can't go to BiLo and get a Butterball out of the freezer section if he comes up short."

Sean finished narrating the coyote's life history, ecology, food habits, risks, and realities. He'd been standing with his arms hugging Scooter for about ten minutes. Finally he said, "I think it's time we put him up."

Sean and Scooter have formed a bond of trust and reciprocal need across the species frontier for two years. Watching them I couldn't help but think about the wolves around our fires, and about all the other animals we have domesticated through the ages. Did it always start this way? With connection? With care? But wildness exists separate from us. I could still sense it in Scooter. I remembered Flag and Prairie and River and how this liminal space between wild and tame is a hard one to negotiate and maintain. I wished this continuing experiment in cross-species community the best, and I hoped at some point there would be hundreds of educational coyotes in schools throughout the South.

Before I put down my notebook, I wrote one more thought. Though this isn't a circus, Sean was still a sort of lion trainer. Sean had taught Scooter a few dog tricks, like sitting every night before he gives him his raw deer treat. But there is more to what Sean and Scooter are doing than an act. I could see it in the way Sean stood hugging Scooter for that final minute before the coyote went back into the kennel, and I could see it also in the way Scooter rotated his head to look at the children sitting before him. His long nose was an arrow pointing both to the distance separating us, and to what connects us.

In a dream one night I was presented with two coyotes, a black male who lunged in to nip from a leash's end, and a white female who never bit but lunged just the same. Wonder is not a disease, Alan Watts reminded us. I want to make sure I express the wonder I feel for coyotes, the wonder that they have survived, that they have prospered, that they will somehow be with us now forever unless somehow they are wiped out by some pathogen. Rachel Carson said, "A child's world is fresh and new and beautiful, full of wonder and excitement. It is our misfortune that for most of us that clear-eyed vision, that true instinct for what is beautiful and awe-inspiring, is dimmed and even lost before we reach adulthood," and as if to confirm Carson's legacy, the little girl who was afraid of snakes said, "He's a very pretty animal." In the moment before Scooter disappeared back into his kennel she added, "I like the color of his hair."

Beyond the Reach of the Loudspeakers

The higher the intelligence of any species, the more vari-
ations in behavior among its individuals. The degree of
their uniformity is in ratio to their stupidity.
—J. Frank Dobie

In mid-June I made arrangements to meet John Kilgo at his
office at the U.S Forest Service complex a mile inside the barrier on
the 310-square-mile Savannah River Site back down in Aiken. I had
unfinished business. I wanted to find out all I could about the science
behind our coyotes. I wanted to sort through some of what we really
know and what we don't know about the coyotes settling the South.

In the early 1950s the SRS began fabricating nuclear weapons; today,
the site is mostly in cleanup mode and none of the reactors are oper-
ational, though several of the areas are used to store nuclear waste.
Though nuclear fabrication has been scaled back in the sprawling facility there is active forest management on the site, and the University
of Georgia still operates the Savannah River Ecology Lab, open since
1951, where some of the longest running environmental research in the
world on radiation and population dynamics has taken place. Still, to
visit SRS I'd needed to secure a badge, a procedure that required two
IDs, and submit to an inspection of every compartment of my vehicle. The inspection went well. The guard was friendly, though heavily
armed, a civilian contractor dressed in camo who wore a floppy jungle
hat like a special ops soldier.

John has been a researcher for the U.S. Forest Service for two decades. He had a bear paw sculpture for an office doorstop, a large deer skull mounted on the wall, collages of family photos, a framed picture of two almost invisible fawns bedded down in brush, and a poster announcing an ivory bill woodpecker conference on his door.

The deer skull showed John's love for deer hunting, the grizzly bear paw cast demonstrated his love for the West, the photos of family illustrated his loyalty, the fawns, one of his primary research interests as a biologist, and the ivory bill poster made a lasting connection to his father (and my friend), the late James Kilgo, whose memoir *Deep Enough for Ivorybills* probes the edges of southern wilderness and hunting culture better than just about anything published, except maybe William Faulkner's "The Bear."

John would appreciate my reference to Faulkner. He was almost a double major in English and biology at Wofford College, where I teach and where his father attended. I was even John's teacher once, as I sponsored a January independent class John and several friends had designed to visit and explore natural areas across South Carolina, including mountain waterfalls. That class almost turned tragic as one day a call from John's dad, Jim, informed me John had fallen off a frozen waterfall and walked out three miles to meet an ambulance at the highway. John recovered and went on to get his masters at the University of Florida and his PhD in wildlife biology at the University of Georgia. From there, he began a long career as a wildlife researcher, starting with neotropical birds, then moving on to work on the deer and coyote questions that interested me. He's worked on the Savannah River Site since he was a graduate student in 1992 and he knows it intimately. The site is one of his home landscapes, and I imagine it pleased his father to no end that he had settled into research in the piney woods and floodplain forests of South Carolina's upper coastal plain.

John is quiet, with a sharp intelligence and sense of humor that surfaces when he relaxes and begins telling stories associated with his research. He's spent thousands of hours in the field and often, as we all know, that sort of intimate contact with wildness leaves one open to see and experience interesting things. On the day I visited SRS John was dressed in a khaki shirt and field boots, and he looked a little like his dad's author photo on the flap of *Deep Enough for Ivorybills*, though John has more blond hair and no facial hair at the moment. A shared, fierce seriousness is present in both the eyes of father and son. James Kilgo was forty-seven when his first book came out. John is forty-seven now, already far into an admirable career as a wildlife biologist.

I'd come to talk coyotes, and so we settled down in John's office for an hour before he would drive me around the fifty-year-old Department of Energy site (what used to be known as the bomb—or "bum"—plant to locals). John wanted to show me the three study areas where he and his team had worked, the landscape that had led to several important papers on coyote–deer interactions.

As we sat John explained he got interested in deer and coyotes when it became clear in the late 1990s that deer numbers in South Carolina had started to decline. I remembered a simple graph I had seen in one of John's articles that described the relationship between fawns/does and coyotes, at least on the Savannah River Site. On the left end of the graph was the number of surviving fawns per doe, from 0 to 1.4. The x-axis showed the forty years from 1965 to 2005. The number of fawns peaked about 1969 at about 1.3 and then fluctuated but stayed steady until 1989 from between 1.3 and a little over 1.0. In 1989 a decline began, and by 2005 the number of fawns per doe was down to 0.3. The right axis registered coyotes, from "few" to "many." That line is still headed straight upward from its origin about 1987, the first record of a coyote on SRS.

Deer management literature at first said, "don't shoot the does," and then it said, "shoot as many does as you can," but, as John explained, "hunters got used to the numbers of deer they saw in the eighties and nineties—then the coyotes showed up and deer got the double whammy."

"But why is there so much interest in coyotes?"

"Soon as something impacts you directly—whether it's your livelihood or your hobby—you start noticing," John said.

If you are not one to read John's scientific papers, it doesn't mean you haven't heard about the conclusions of his research. State departments of natural resources, message boards, and bulletins have circulated John's team's findings about fawn predation all over the region. Coyotes are killing a lot of deer fawns. On YouTube there are 5,300 videos uploaded under the key words "coyote killing fawn." These videos are often scored with dramatic classical music like Beethoven's Fifth Symphony in order to heighten the suspense of all this fawn killing, most often caught on the now cheap and ubiquitous game cameras. Images from these cameras now catch coyotes hauling off fawns all over the South.

The emotional and sociological issues associated with deer-killing coyotes are hard to sort through. Hunters everywhere will tell you there aren't enough deer, and herd numbers have fallen after a peak in most states in the 1990s. Homeowners in the suburbs say they have more than enough deer when the hydrangeas and hostas start to disappear, nibbled to nonflowering nubs in early summer. Deer–car collisions cost insurance companies billions of dollars and kill many people. Environmental writer Jim Minick presents a common perspective in a piece he wrote for *Oxford American*: "Scientists have extensively documented what a [national] population of 30 million deer do to our country's landscape . . . 'what was once a species-rich and lush understory of forbs and shrubs [turns] into a depauperate understory dominated by a few ferns, grasses, and browse-resistant trees.' It takes many, many decades for the forest to recover. Put another way: we are drowning in deer."

Though this sounds like an antihunting essay, Jim Minick is not a classic deer hugger. This quote comes from the middle of a powerful piece he wrote about having to drown a wounded deer he had shot, and his hopes to cut up and fill his freezer with the meat. "My wife and I eat one deer a year, or usually less. Our dogs eat all we can give."

What to do with all our deer and how to manage them/kill them/ hug them, whatever you want to call our relationship, is a question as complex as they come. Jim Minick says kill and eat all we can. Many hunters would agree with him. In 2013 in South Carolina alone, hunters shot (and probably ate, or will thaw and eat) 225,000 deer of an estimated 800,000 deer herd. One website calls South Carolina "deer friendly," and it's probably because the economic and cultural impact of deer hunting is huge—hundreds of millions of dollars. With numbers like this, it's good to be seen as "deer friendly."

The presence of coyotes presents an answer to the deer question that is even more vexing. At the same time that South Carolina deer hunters are reporting they harvested a quarter-million deer in 2013 they also say they killed about thirty thousand coyotes in South Carolina. The coyote number has grown each year since the 1990s, up over 6 percent this year alone, though SCDNR claims the population is now leveling off. This translates in South Carolina into the death of almost one and a half coyotes per square mile of the Palmetto State. If this is true, it's a miracle we don't trip over a coyote every time we go into the yard, the woods, or the mall.

Mostly what people remember from John's coyote research is not the important new data on range, food habits, or reproduction, but the percentage of fawns killed by coyotes in his SRS zones each of the three years—77 percent of all fawns born die somehow within their first three months; 80 percent of those deaths are from coyotes, and so 62 percent of all fawns born are killed by coyotes. One of my primary questions for John has to do with how state agencies use scientific data to encourage hunters to shoot coyotes and the public's willingness to extrapolate his data outward over the entire South. I pulled what several biologists have referred to as "the wanted poster" from my backpack. Soon after John's research was published, scDNR printed and distributed these posters in game check stations, taxidermy shops, and hunting stores. The poster shows a scary coyote, ears laid back in midflight, ready to pounce on a running fawn. "Hunters Help Control Coyotes. Save our Deer!" the headline exclaims. There are seven bullet points superimposed on the chase scene—including the numbers on fawn mortality drawn from John's work—56 percent of fawns "preyed upon by coyotes."

John looked over the poster. "I've seen this online," he said, and nodded.

"Is the information accurate?" I asked.

"That's close to our average here over three years," he said after reading the text, but then he singled out one of the points encouraging intensive trapping to increase fawn survival. "But our data showed that trapping on srs had no effect on the coyote population, though other studies elsewhere may have produced different results."

I pushed the issue a little about the line between science and government. "Isn't a poster like this over the top?"

"There aren't many brand new wildlife issues in the Southeast. Coyotes are one. No one believes deer are going extinct, but when hunters see fewer deer they ask, 'What's going on?' That's when scDNR jumps on board."

"Will this coyote issue become less emotional over time?"

"Once again, it isn't a typical issue. Though there are pythons in South Florida, not many would argue for the place of pythons in those ecosystems. Some would argue for coyotes and that they belong here. A parallel may be with wolves out west. There's a large predator that belongs—but still, wolves are tremendously divisive and a complicated social issue."

"Will these posters someday come down?"

"I would hope so, but there are people out west who want every wolf dead. And I don't believe everyone at DNR is completely happy about this poster either. When I say DNR I mean the biologists, and I have a lot of respect for DNR biologists."

I had a lot to think about. Though coyotes are known by biologists as generalist predators, I knew from reading that the often larger eastern coyotes can and will kill and eat deer, if given the chance, and today they have plenty of chances. Coyotes have settled this region (the American South) at the opportune time, at the same historic moment that the white-tailed deer has become firmly reestablished in the second-, third-, and fourth-growth forests, the fields, the sustaining suburbs, and even the urban areas like Atlanta and Charlotte. By great numbers of deer, I mean really big numbers. Millions. If you build the herd, they will come. And if they come, some predator won't be far behind.

Single coyotes probably don't often pursue adult deer, and they rarely, if ever, make a kill. Pairs of coyotes will pursue deer and, as the research shows, at least in the Northeast, are fairly successful at making kills. Coyotes will also work in cooperation with larger groups of coyotes; these groups can and will run deer down, kill them, and then feed upon them. Even if larger groups of coyotes kill deer it may or may not be appropriate to refer to them as a "pack," though you will see the term used quite widely in popular literature and on the web. Packs are associated most often with wolves and suggest complex, refined social structures. Coyote social groups are probably temporary, often extended families. Coyotes are not wolves. Primarily they hunt alone, but they also hunt in these temporary social groups.

The coyote cousins, the wolves, are carnivores. Coyotes eat almost everything—so they are classified as omnivores, like crows, chickens, some lizards and turtles, opossums, squirrels, skunks, raccoons, rats, bears, and of course, us. A coyote diet, through the year, has a great abundance of available wild fruit—most seasons, except winter, the vast majority of the coyote scat researchers find contains the seeds of various fruit—pokeberries, plums, blackberries, and persimmons to name a few. Coyotes are so general in their food habits that when one food source diminishes, they'll simply switch. If there are plums, they'll eat plums. If the deer are too fast to catch, they'll catch lizards, mice, and grasshoppers, even eat roadkill.

If a hungry coyote gets lucky and stumbles upon a sick or injured adult deer, it will try to kill it and eat it. As I said, they kill deer. There isn't any denying that. They also eat an occasional calf or goat, sheep, small dog or cat, insects, eggs, watermelons, and other cultivated fruit. No denying that either.

Though coyotes killing an adult deer in the South is probably a rare thing, I imagine it happens here in a similar way as it happens elsewhere. Coyotes cross a deer trail and follow it. They may chase and bring down the animal by pursuit. Most likely the deer will get away. If the coyotes do get close enough, they'll hamstring the prey or nip at the deer's haunches; they'll do whatever they need to do as efficient hunters to slow the deer down and get it on the ground. Then the coyotes may try to dispatch the deer quickly by biting at its throat. Killing an adult deer for a coyote is a very dangerous process. A full-grown deer likely does not go gently into that good night. Deer fight like hell, kicking mostly. Richard Nelson in *Heart and Blood*, his book about deer in America, says deer are good matches for coyotes, and he doubts coyotes have much effect on deer populations when it comes to killing adult deer.

Most of the deer killed by coyotes in the South (and probably elsewhere as well) are fawns, and they are often killed during the very vulnerable period right after birth, corresponding in the South to the late spring and early summer. This is the time of year we could think of as ideal for an opportunistic omnivore with small passive pure protein packages nested conveniently throughout their range—like having a McDonald's on every corner.

Through the literary devices of irony and analogy (the processed food image and the McDonald's) I made the fawn predation clever and funny, though the idea of coyotes killing fawns is not a pleasant one to imagine. We don't know exactly how the coyotes locate fawns. They could key on does, systematically search for the newborns, or just stumble upon them; as the does deliver or a few hours or days after, coyotes dispatch the fawns with a bite to top of the skull like eating a cherry tomato, and they often consume the fawn on site, cache it (by burying the carcass), or haul the fawn off to a rendezvous site or a den site to feed their own growing coyote pups.

Without coyotes what's called "fawn recruitment" was pretty good all over the South, but many factors work against fawn survival in that first few months such as abandonment, car fatalities, accidents, and occasional predation by other animals, including hogs, bobcats, bears, foxes, and domestic dogs. If a car hits a fawn's mother, the fawn is left to fend for itself. Just this week (early June, as I write this) a friend picked up a doe, dead by the side of the road, and noticed she'd been lactating when she was killed. That next morning a desperate fawn tried to nurse from a large docile dog in a nearby yard.

Like John, many researchers in the South have documented the fact of fawn predation by coyotes. As early as the 1990s researchers in Alabama, Kentucky, Mississippi, and Tennessee began looking at the summer diet of coyotes. Through scat and stomach analysis they found coyotes in what they called "high density deer areas" were eating deer, and a majority of those deer were fawns. More specific research on fawn predation by coyotes followed, and my former student John Kilgo and others did some of the earliest and highest profile work on the Savannah River Site.

After our discussion we still had a trip into the field, so John showed me out the door to his green Forest Service pickup. We climbed in and went to gas up first. John called in to alert security of his itinerary, and I asked about the call. "You're supposed to tell them every time you move. It's called 'The Remote Worker Tracking System.' Anybody beyond the reach of the loudspeakers is supposed to communicate."

I told John I liked it that we would be "beyond the reach of the loud-speakers," and he laughed. There was something interesting about that metaphor, something that seemed to fit with coyotes and deer, and wildness, and science, and a tract of land the size of some European countries. Science researchers like John should always be beyond the reach of the loudspeakers, no matter who is broadcasting over them—DNRS, other government agencies, private citizens, even writers like me. The posters represent a loudspeaker for the fears of DNR board members and frightened hunters. Anyone taking the time to read John's research could see a more complex picture of the whole coyote issue in the South.

We were soon on the road, and John had brought a map along to help me visualize the location of his three study areas. I looked down at the white paper expanse divided into ninety-two "compartments" and how they were covered with roads, transmission lines, several rail-roads, perennial and intermittent streams, canals and ditches, lakes, the Savannah River, and the orange areas called "facilities" where the dirty nuclear work had taken place all those years. There were five or six of these orange areas.

I could see the SRS was no roadless wilderness. The only area without a significant system of roads crossing it was the one labeled "92" in the south, the ten-mile-long floodplain of the river. I asked John about the intricate system of gravel capillaries—the tiny black lines on the map—crisscrossing the official "Remote Worker Map," and he explained how many of the roads predated the establishment of the SRS but were used extensively for the forest management program. "Preserving the wilderness was never an objective here," he said.

John stopped the truck where a power line crossed the gravel road. To our right was a large thicket of wild plums. "This is what the coyotes are eating mostly right now, mostly in these power right-of-ways. The hogs are eating them too," John explained. Hundreds of small plums hung heavy from brown-and-white-dappled branches of the sprawling thicket. I got out and looked under the bushes. There were many hog and coyote tracks intermingled in the dried mud where they had been grazing on the limbs, eating the cherry-red fruit from among the fingers of green leaves.

"Can I eat one?" I asked.

"I must officially tell you that you are not supposed to," John said.

John has deployed as many as eighty trailcams at a time, so he's seen plenty of digital coyotes—walking down the roads in shadowy night visions, peeing on fatty acid tablets the researchers put out as bait in vivid color, carrying dead fawns, and even once hauling a deer head complete with antlers. Based on the number of coyotes trapped in his three sectors of the srs John can say that the coyote population here locally is stable and dense—and his project's trapping seemed to have little impact on the population. "Each year we took off one hundred and fifty to one hundred and seventy coyotes for three years—almost five hundred over three years. You do the math—four to five per square mile for three years in a row. The contract trappers were taking off as many at the end of the study as they were at the beginning. Can deer hunters shoot one or two per square mile in a season and not affect the coyote population? Absolutely."

We drove from zone 1 to zone 2, where the researchers had done much of their work with does and fawns. We pulled into a clearing that had once been a food plot established to trap turkeys for transplant elsewhere in the 1970s. As the truck idled, John explained the basic premises and mechanics of their research. In late winter they darted does and equipped the sedated animals with radio collars and inserted vits (vaginal implant transmitters). These two transmitters would tell them the location of the does and when the fawns were born. As John put it, "The whole point of doe capture was fawn capture."

The vit transmitters were relatively new when John started his research and used them the first time in 2006. "We started playing with them in 2002. We implanted a doe and found two fawns. They've only had widespread use in the last ten years. The first papers started appearing around 2008."

Once the fawns were born they were located and fitted with their own collars. None of this was simple work. John and his colleagues used some of these new technologies (such as the night goggles and DNA sampling) for the first time in the region, and often the success or failure was hit and miss. First they tried to catch the does with rocket nets (nets fired over a clearing). They initially caught a number of deer with this technique, but their success waned. Then they tried dart guns in which the dart had the transmitter for tracking the deer. They didn't get many deer that way either. Dart guns aren't very accurate, especially since you are shooting at night and often using a night vision scope. But over time they got it down to an art.

"This spot was especially productive," John said as we looked out at the clearing in the forest.

Once they darted a doe and it was rereleased, someone had to check the radio for signals every eight hours during the fawning season. "The implant beeps normally when inside the deer, but when it comes out the pulse rate changes—beep, beep, beep . . . We'll know deer number such-and-such has dropped. The code tells you how long it's been, and two or three people have to go and find the fawn. If you get there quick enough the fawn is still lying there. But if it's been five or six hours, it becomes a search. When you arrive you want to approach from downwind. We go to the doe first. If we get lucky she jumps and runs—and there's the fawn. If not, we search with the thermal scope—picking up body heat—any animal will glow white hot.

"The first two or three weeks a fawn's survival strategy is hiding— once you find them it's not hard to catch them. You just reach down and pick them up."

Does, John explained, will have two fawns, "eighty percent of the time, roughly." It was hard going finding does before the transmitters were invented. "Big crews would just get out and look for them—that way it would be really, really hard to find enough fawns for a study, especially in the South, where the cover is so dense."

They check the fawn collars several times a day, sometimes for several weeks. When the collar hasn't moved for four hours they switch to "mortality" mode, which is detected by a change in the beep sequence.

"Basically it just starts to beep really fast," John said. "Then we track the collar down and there's the dead fawn."

Once the dead fawn is located, it turns into what John calls "a CSI crime scene." They take samples to run to locate the predator's DNA. (Eighty percent of the dead fawns have coyote DNA on them.) "When I first started I didn't even know I could get residual saliva and determine species."

Sometimes there is only a radio collar left. Sometimes only a bone fragment. John describes what he calls "a classic coyote kill": the coyote digs a hole and buries what's left. Bobcats will also cover their kill, but they don't disturb the dirt. Coyotes kill and then dig, and cover with twigs and dirt. "We still don't know how coyotes find fawns, but I suspect the coyotes often find them in their beds. They catch them there and just crunch down."

As we headed back to his office John talked a little more about what he knew of the SRS coyotes. They are highly variable in their behavior, and therefore fit Dobie's definition of high levels of intelligence. There seem to be trends in their visibility. In the late nineties John would see coyotes much more often. There are more of them now, but "you don't see them anymore. They've probably learned they're being persecuted."

By persecution I knew John meant trapping and hunting, and by this definition, they'd done some serious persecution. The research had employed three trappers a year for three years, and in the research zones they'd removed the 474 coyotes John had mentioned before, "reducing coyote abundance by seventy-eight percent from pre-removal levels" during the month of May, shortly after trapping. Unfortunately, the survival of the fawns in the study areas did not increase over time as the coyotes were killed. The survival rate was best the first year, but it dropped through the next two years of the study. After the research concluded, John and his team wrote up their findings. At the end of their abstract they stated that the removal of the coyotes as a strategy for increasing fawn recruitment does not seem viable, though the idea warrants more study.

Despite the persecution, John's research helps confirm the future is looking pretty bright for coyotes. They have to be smart, but they are survivors. "One hundred and fifty years of coyote persecution and what do we have now?" John asked. "Not fewer coyotes, but coyotes all over the continent."

"Here are some coyotes," John said, placing miniature clear vials with black lids on the crowded desk once we are back in the office. Something multiple, tiny, and white floated in each.

"Coyote teeth?" I asked.

"No, fetuses," he said.

They had been extracted from autopsied females in the coyote-trapping project as part of their data gathering. "There were an average of four or five. In one female we could see placental scars for up to eleven but no way to tell whether she carried them to term."

I picked up one vial and swirled it, and a line of tiny white curled coyotes with dark purple umbilical cords still attached danced upward through the clear liquid. I tried to comprehend what I was seeing— ghost dogs? a tiny ghoulish can-can? sleeping siblings of a lost SRS generation in motion? poetic cousins to cave fish?—and then through a strange association from my literary past I remembered James Dickey's poem "The Sheep-Child," one of the archetypal southern images of human–animal relations gone way too far, the haunting story of a boy shown a bleached white fetus, a nightmare, half sheep, half human, stored on the dusty back shelf of an Atlanta museum.

In Dickey's poem the pickled sheep-child speaks, telling of his brief hybrid life as he is birthed "in the long grass of the west pasture . . . /

Listening for foxes," where he is suckled, and quickly dies, "because / Those things can't live." Dickey says he wrote the poem to articulate "the enormous need for contact that runs through all of sentient nature, and has no regard whatever for boundaries of species."

Watching the fetuses dance elicited sympathy in me for the coyotes but also sympathy for the SRS fawns born yearly out in the woods— their brief lives and how their only contact with another species comes in a swift attack with a fatal bite most often to their fragile skulls. I know it's not what Dickey meant exactly, but these coyotes are a product of their intimate interactions with us over time. We made the landscape that created success for them. We have been foster parents to their pioneering success with our vast alterations of both landscape and biome. We are responsible both for them, now, and for what we have made.

The tiny coyotes settled back into place. This was a new way for me to see coyotes, suspended in clear liquid, studied, stockpiled, and I found the opportunity fascinating, but more than a little unsettling. John had his biological training to hold such hauntings at bay. Though I did not ask him, he could probably suspend such poetic thoughts, focusing on what could be learned from the trapped coyotes and their body parts. There was little if any room on the autopsy sheet or the peer-reviewed paper built from observation, evaluation, and synthesis for poetic allusions. That was up to me.

Outlaw Coyote

Coyote never dies, he gets killed plenty of times, but
always comes back to life again, and then he goes right
on traveling.—Gary Snyder

The lives of animals are good to use to think about our own
lives. They provide us with rich symbols to pour our deepest experiences into, and they can become vessels for understanding our
complex, evolving human world. True events and encounters quickly
become stories passed on for meaning. Coyotes survive as both real
animals migrating east and as mythic and folkloric characters, even as
a mass-market pop culture cartoon character now forever locked in
mock battle with the roadrunner on YouTube.

The stories people tell about coyotes are mostly about how surprised—or surprising—their appearance happens to be. The hunter
might say, the coyote did such and such a thing. Coyotes always seem
to be underappreciated, little understood, and always unpredictable.
Unlike out west, there aren't many stories yet in the South about living with them. But in this way the coyote provides southerners with
a way to think about change, about time, and about our resistance to
both—and how systems may have already altered, changed without
our noticing, which may be one of our private forms of denial.

Nobody knows how the outlaw coyote got to West Virginia. Some
think it was transplanted from the West as a pup, maybe brought in by
fox hunters or kept as a pet and released after the owner was unable to

tame it. In 1970 there were rarely three or four free-ranging coyotes in the state at any given time.

A local West Virginia Department of Natural Resources trapper was probably the first to see the tawny predator and identify it not as a feral dog but as a rare West Virginia coyote. He'd trapped problem bears, beavers, and minks all over the state, but this animal sure roused his interest. For the first few months the coyote slipped out on efforts of the trapper and his colleagues to catch it, and it began to worry the local sheep farmers. Sometimes a farmer would see it during the day mingling with his sheep and then wake up frustrated to find the outlaw had returned to kill after dark.

During that first year on the lam, the outlaw coyote sidestepped traps that the DNR trappers and the sheep farmers set for it. Sometimes the coyote covered them with leaves and sticks, and other times it deposited its droppings beside them. It swam rivers and lakes, crept along fence lines, and doubled back on its own trail whenever it was pursued, which was often.

The DNR trappers tried hunting alone. Then they paired off to follow dogs along the hogback ridges of that northeast corner of West Virginia. They wanted one clear shot, but the chance came only occasionally and they always missed. There was the feeling that the coyote was watching the hunt, standing just out of sight, obscured by the deep tree cover of the West Virginia mountains or the boulders on the hillsides. Once the men on a fresh trail watched the outlaw coyote race out of a sewer pipe and swim across a pond to get away like a hero from an English highwayman ballad. Another time one of the trappers jumped the coyote on a rock ledge in an old strip mine. The trapper saw the outlaw coyote slumbering at the top. He rustled a branch and the coyote woke, sprang to its feet, and sped away as the trapper filled the air with misplaced lead.

The outlaw coyote grew larger than life. It stepped beyond the bounds of natural history, approaching folklore, tall-tale hero, or cartoon canine. It was like Lord Randall or John Barleycorn or Robin Hood. But this maverick coyote was a loner and shared none of his spoils—a mounting toil of sheep—with its band of Merry Men.

A year passed, and the chase continued. The local trappers surmised they were dealing with one male coyote, as they figured a female would have tried to mate with a dog when in heat, her natural wariness overcome by a deep need for procreation.

The West Virginia DNR brought in a Kansas tracker with specially bred coyote dogs, but, used to flat Kansas prairie, the special dogs soon lost their way in the West Virginia hills and disappeared; one was found days later, seventy-five miles distant near the Ohio River. Sometimes the coyote heard the trackers' dogs coming and fell in behind a herd of deer. Once the dogs followed the coyote into a herd of cattle, and an overzealous farmer shot up his own herd. A total of twenty-one dogs were mistaken for the outlaw and shot. Only once did a foxhound catch up with him. The next morning tracks in the snow showed how the coyote stopped, circled, and prepared to make a stand before the overmatched dog fled.

The Kansas tracker said, "That coyote will stand on the next hill to see whether you've got a shotgun or a rifle. You're chasing a four-footed computer."

As if on cue, the outlaw coyote showed himself out of range and then disappeared into the woods.

Rewards did no good. The sheep killing continued. Finally, the local authorities called in the state. After the first snowfall the hunt intensified. The state wardens hunted daily.

And then the air assault began. The National Guard called in a helicopter, and Consolidated Gas provided two airplanes. For the first time permits were allowed in West Virginia for aerial shooting, and the pilots flew fifty feet off the tree line. A farmer and his two sons were spreading manure when a helicopter roared low just over their heads. "As we looked back," one of the searchers in the helicopter reported, "all we could see were the boys face down in the manure and the old man's feet sticking out from under the spreader."

Suggestions for bagging the outlaw came in from everywhere. Someone said to add glue to the traps. Someone else suggested that "love and kindness" would convince the outlaw to give up. He seemed to thrive on the chase, to grow bolder the more he was pursued.

Then in late April of 1970 the DNR trappers had one more idea. They brought in a nine-year-old captive female coyote in heat from out west. They placed her on top of a hill above a sheep farm in Hacker's Creek Valley north of the town of Buckhanan, where, as a local newspaper put it, "she held court under the April moon."

Hacker's Creek runs bold as it meanders through open fields bordered by steep ridges. Old red barns look ready for rural life posters. Along the road there are still more pickups than sedans.

Tracks the first morning showed the outlaw coyote had approached the caged female bedded down on straw. Tracks in a late snow showed he approached but backed off. The next night the men from the wildlife department decided to scatter the female coyote's straw bedding leading to the trap area, and about 2:00 a.m. the coyote approached the female and stepped in a trap, dragging it three hundred yards until the chain was tangled in a barbed wire fence. That next morning the farmer on whose land the animal was found dispatched the outlaw coyote with a single shot through the heart.

The killing spree was beyond belief—a thousand dead sheep worth $75,000, plus all the resources spent to bring the outlaw to bay. "The presence of this remarkable animal has not been lost," reported "The Coyote That Outfoxed a Whole State," an article published forty-four years ago about the coyote hunt in *True* magazine. "If your travels ever take you to the West Virginia foothills, stop off at the French Creek Game Farm and right in the middle of the lobby stands a mount of the maverick coyote."

While searching for stories to help me understand the outlaw coyote I stumbled upon a brief line of comment by writer Wendell Berry about coyotes coming into the country around his Kentucky farm. In a letter to Gary Snyder written in March of 1989 Berry says, "We have coyotes now, did I tell you? They like lamb. We have a dog who will stay with sheep this time around, which may solve the problem. Let the coyotes eat groundhogs!"

A few years later, in 1993, Jordan Fisher Smith conducted an interview with Wendell Berry and brought up coyotes when the conversation turned to community, and Berry commented: "So the communities have to begin to ask what they need that can be produced locally, by local people and from the local landscape, and how it can be produced in a way that doesn't damage the local landscape or the local community. And by local community, obviously, you can't mean just the people. You mean the people and the natural communities that are supposed to exist there—the trees, the grasses, the animals, the birds, and so on. Everything has to be included and considered."

Fisher Smith countered: "But I notice that there is not much of a constituency for coyotes in this part of Kentucky, especially around your sheep. The restoration of populations of wolves is not a popular idea in the cattle country of the Northern Rockies, and I've seen sea lions and otters dead from gunshot wounds along the Pacific coast fishing grounds, all the way from California to Alaska. How do you address this apparent failing, in practice, of the stewardship ethic you are proposing? Such an ethic seems to favor those things for which you have, what you call, 'affection.'"

Berry responded thoughtfully, and at considerable length: "Well, we obviously have to enlarge affection so that it includes more than those things that are most congenial or profitable. . . . If the coyotes are getting your sheep, as experience has shown, a very impractical approach is to say, 'Well, we'll just kill all the coyotes,' because you're not going to kill them all. They seem to be a species that thrives on human malevolence. A better question is how can you raise sheep in spite of the coyotes, and there are ways of doing that. Here we use donkeys and a guard dog, some electric fence, and we're saving our sheep. All kinds of questions are involved in any of these issues, but the important thing to me is to define the issue with a due regard for its real complexities. The inherited approach to this kind of problem in America is that if you're in the sheep business and coyotes eat sheep, then you must kill coyotes. But that isn't corrected by adopting the opposite one. The opposite approach espoused by some environmentalists is that if you like coyotes and there's a conflict between coyotes and sheep, you ought to kill the sheep. The necessary, and the most interesting, question is how these two things can exist together. It may be that in some places this effort ought to be given up. I thought when the coyotes came in here that this might be one of those places."

After I read Berry's comments to Snyder and to Fisher Smith I wrote to him to ask a follow-up question about coyotes, and he graciously answered, "There is not much use in sentimentalizing our relationship to the 'wild animals.' The coyotes as predators have to be dealt with short of total war, in which victory anyhow seems impossible."

I thought long and hard about what Berry had said and imagined the 1970 outlaw coyote as a sort of harbinger of ideas and issues to come. What can we learn from this isolated case of one sheep-killing coyote? We can learn that a single coyote gone bad, like a mass murderer, can turn a community on its head. We can learn that wild animals are smart, and one might just be smart enough to avoid all control. Best of all, we can see, as Berry suggests, that it might be good to learn to coexist over time, despite our differing desires.

Of the stern warnings I received while writing this book one of the most common was Berry's, to be careful not to sentimentalize coyotes. I've parsed the differences between sympathy and sentiment many times and find the line hard to locate, especially with coyotes, as with all social animals like us. Berry has discussed the idea of how hard it is define animals as "wild" when they do domestic things just like humans, such as establish "homes" and "home ranges," raise families, even, in the case of some of E. O. Wilson's ants, farm. Sharing these traits with animals makes us sympathize with them even more.

One thing I love about the outlaw coyote story is how bold, how heroic, how strong he seems in the face of human action. But this is not out of the ordinary. In traditional coyote stories there is a propensity for the mythic animal to endure all hardships brought on either by his nature or by those opposed to him. In these stories (and even in the cartoons) Coyote always survives. Living as he does on the margins to begin with, there is no need for Coyote to endure at the center of things.

One question that fascinated me about the outlaw coyote story was whether he was still up there, living on as a taxidermy mount in the lobby of a game park in West Virginia. So I did some snooping and called the French Creek wildlife park. The woman on the other end of the line was patient with my long lead-in to what I wanted. "There was a coyote killed there over forty years ago," I said. "I've read the stuffed carcass might still be in your building."

"That old coyote?" the woman said, laughing. "Yeah, he's still here. He's right outside the women's bathroom downstairs."

Of all the stories I'd read or heard about coyotes coming into the South, the one about the outlaw coyote had kept my interest the longest, and I was excited to think I might find some closure on coyotes in general on a road trip, so I talked Mike Willis into heading north with me. Since stumbling upon the reference to the 1970 incident in a footnote I'd chased down the one article in the defunct men's magazine, maybe not the best source, but a source nonetheless.

The story as presented by *True* seemed an entertaining tall tale at best, sort of the hunting and trapping equivalent of "The One That Got Away," narrating a single coyote on an eighteen-month killing spree, dispatching "more than a thousand" sheep, running a pack of dogs ragged, and in the end, defeating the West Virginia National Guard's helicopters and airplanes. I knew it was a good story, and every time I told it to those interested in my coyote project they understood the narrative power of a good outlaw yarn. By the time Mike and I had left for West Virginia I could not remember whether or not the coyote jumped off a rock cliff and swum a lake, or whether they'd staked out the amorous female in the clearing, or whether she'd remained in a cage. As I told the story to friends, I embellished as needed. I'd hoped that seeing the remains of the real coyote mounted in front of the women's bathroom at the game park would give me some certainty in the story, and if I were lucky I might even find someone who could confirm the few ancient, mildewed details I'd gleaned.

We left the interstate at the Flatwoods exit and took to the back roads. The West Virginia landscape didn't look like I imagined sheep country—instead of open range we passed rolling wooded hills, trailers and small frame houses, many old played-out farms, and a few poor pastures—but a lot can change in forty years.

At the wildlife park in French Creek we paid our three-dollar entry fee each to walk if we had time among captive animals kept in large caged enclosures—deer, elk, bears, even coyotes. This place had been a tourist draw for many decades, opening in the 1920s as a sort of zoo, but I hoped the incident with the outlaw coyote would still be fresh in someone's memory.

As the woman gave me my change I said, "What we're really here to see is that stuffed coyote. Which building is he in?"

The attendant gave me a blank stare. "Stuffed coyote?"

"You know, the coyote that outfoxed a whole state?" I said.

"I don't know anything about a stuffed coyote. The DNR headquarters is that brown building over there. Ask them."

We drove over and walked in the building's first floor and looked around until I found the women's restroom. No stuffed coyote in a plastic display box. I was crestfallen and feared I was either in the wrong place or somehow in the months since I'd talked to the woman at the center the coyote had been landfilled in the agency's spring cleaning.

"I'm looking for the stuffed sheep-killing coyote," I said, standing upstairs before a man answering email at a desk. "Danny Reed," the man said, introducing himself, and I remembered that he was the DNR supervisor, and I'd talked to him on the phone. He didn't seem surprised at my request, as if people came in often to ask about the stuffed coyote. We shook hands and he said, "We've moved him. We'll have to go over to another building. Follow me."

We walked out the back. "Well, looka there. It's your lucky day," Danny said. "It's Clyde Campbell and Ray Heffner. There's who you need to talk to."

At the bottom of the steps two men stood talking in the parking lot. I recognized Clyde's name from the article. I knew I'd hit the jackpot.

Ray is the quieter of the two. He is tall and slender, blue jeans, red checkerboard button down, stock of elegant white hair. Clyde is a little shorter and more talkative. He was dressed more like a sportsman—camo Cat hat, a Team Realtree golf shirt with camo shoulder panels, and a carved antler belt buckle with a wild turkey on it.

Danny receded from the conversation and took a seat on the steps. I quickly gave Clyde and Ray my spiel about the outlaw coyote and pulled out the *True* article that had brought me north.

"That's that hunter from Kansas with the dogs," Clyde said to Ray when I showed them the photocopy of the forty-two-year-old article from *True*. Clyde pointed down at the dark photo of a pack of dogs and ten men standing in the West Virginia snow decades earlier.

"So you remember the story?" I said.

"Oh, I remember," Clyde said. "Me and Ray trapped him and I shot him over on Hacker's Creek."

"We had quite a time," Ray added.

"That coyote was smart," Clyde said, still studying the picture. "There was a lot of stories but a bunch of them were true."

"It says here the hunter shot him," I said.

"Well, we decided to report it that way to keep me out of trouble with the department," Clyde said, smiling, at the old deception.

"We were in some steep country," Ray said.

"We caught him in the snow," Clyde explained. "We tracked that thing, I'd hate to say how many times. That last winter the ground was frozen. We went from Bracey Fork to Berlin in one day. Right at ten miles."

"He was sharp. I think a farmer shot at him once up on Hacker's Creek," Ray added.

I was trying to recover my bearings, a sort of low-grade shock had set in to be talking to the two men who had tracked and killed the outlaw coyote, not the best frame of mind for an interview. "How did that coyote get here?" I finally asked, stumbling through another question.

"Hard to say," Clyde answered.

"It could have been people ordered foxes and got a coyote with them," Ray said.

"Lot's of people say it got out from the game farm," Clyde said. "But the only thing ever got away from here was a fisher. I've chased down escaped bobcats."

"We run wolves clear to French Creek," Ray said.

"But the only thing that got away was that fisher," Clyde added.

I read Ray and Clyde some more details from the story, like how many sheep it claimed the outlaw coyote had killed, and they both laughed. "No, it wasn't over a thousand," Clyde said, shaking his head. "We were pretty precise with our total. What was it, Ray?"

"Six hundred and something?"

"It's in there on the plaque."

"And it says here he jumped off a rock ledge and swam a lake," I said, misremembering the details.

"Weren't any lakes back then," Ray said.

"When this piece came out I called it 'Believe it or Not,'" Clyde laughed, paging through the three-page photocopy.

"How about the planes and helicopters?" I asked.

"Yeah, we had a helicopter and some planes," Clyde said. "Up there it put you in the mind of a hawk."

"We were in some steep county," Ray repeated.

"What do you remember about how you heard about him the first time?" Mike asked.

"I forgot when we started in on him. People would call and say, 'my sheep was killed last night.' We'd go out and check it, sometimes we could see it was a wild dog killed them but when they had their throats ripped out, we knew it was him."

"Did he eat 'em?" Mike asked.

"He only killed as well as I remember it, and didn't eat any of them."

"He was sharp though," Ray said.

"Remember we got him cornered once but DNR wouldn't let us shoot him because it was Easter Sunday?"

"We had everybody out chasing him, even school kids," Ray added.

"We had a lot of company," Clyde said.

"What kind of hounds were you running?" Mike asked.

"Walker hounds, but one," Ray said.

"And the trap? What did you catch him in?"

"A number three double-spring Victor. I still got it at the house. They told me afterwards they were going to chrome plate it," Clyde said.

"Is it true y'all staked out a female coyote in heat and that's what finally brought him in?" I asked.

"Yes, kept her in her cage, and the first night he came in, but the trap didn't spring. It was mighty cold. Second night we took her straw bedding out, and he came in again and circled the cage and stepped in the trap, and that time we had him," Clyde explained.

"We used a cinch post set," Ray said. "He'd stepped in three sets before but we got him that time."

"The next day we took that dead coyote around to two or three schools," Clyde said.

"What's the coyote situation like up here now?" Mike asked.

"Oh, they're everywhere," Clyde said. "Have been since the eighties."

"Do you hunt them?" Mike asked.

Clyde reached in his pocket and pulled out a tiny bone whistle, put it to his lips and blew. "Hear that? It'll bring 'em in. Sounds like a dying rabbit or a fawn deer. I think everybody should have one."

"Let's go over to see him," I said, and so we followed Danny and Clyde's pickups over to the Natural Resources building where Danny said they'd moved the stuffed coyote.

The big meeting room had a taxidermied wild turkey, a dozen mounted heads—elk, bison, deer, moose—a huge black bear skin tacked on the long wall. In the middle of the same wall stood the Plexiglas box with the outlaw coyote still inside.

I was disappointed but in an understated way when I first saw him. Crouching with his mouth agape, my long-anticipated outlaw coyote's legs looked spindly, and he crouched in such a way that the back ones were bent at unnatural angles. Forty-four years had bleached his pelt a ghostly gray-white. The tip of his tail showed no sign of a black paint-tip, a mark of the species. They'd positioned a little puff of wool with several spots stained slightly pink to represent the 632 sheep the "costly marauder" (as the plaque named him) had actually dispatched.

What did I expect? Something out of the ordinary, but this outlaw looked like every other mounted coyote I'd seen in my travels, only this one was empty of color, unlike the stories that survived. Whatever set him apart from his millions of future cousins now populating the South must have happened inside his skull, or in his coyote genes. It is an extraordinary story, but all that is left of it in the material world of French Creek, West Virginia, is quite common: an aging, bad taxidermy job.

"See that crook in his left foot?" Clyde said, approaching the box and pointing down. I saw what Clyde was pointing out, the fur rubbed raw where his trap had clamped shut that final snowy morning before the West Virginia outlaw coyote's lonely rampage came to an end in the presence of his hopeful suitor, and they all began to tell his story.

Coyote under the Pear Tree

There is no seasoning in the world that can compare with
moral ambiguity.—Seamus McGraw

About the time I heard the coyotes behind our house, my
brother-in-law reported at least three coyotes—two healthy, and one
with an injured foot—eating pears from under a pear tree in his yard
on the edge of the suburbs. He described the injured coyote hopping
up to the tree on three feet and sitting down. The injured animal
sat on its haunches under the tree and looked across the yard at my
brother-in-law as he headed into the house in the late afternoon. After
my brother-in-law spotted the injured animal he texted me, "Should I
kill a wounded coyote hanging out in my yard?"

I didn't get the text right away. When I did, I opened it and wondered if I should text him back and say I wouldn't shoot it. Should I
have released the fate of this particular local coyote to the wind? Should
I have tried to convince my brother-in-law that he needed to tolerate
this wounded coyote visiting the pear buffet in his backyard?

I knew my brother-in-law was a responsible hunter, and so he would
have no trouble taking a shot at a coyote in his yard. Despite our differences about wildlife management, I have tried hard to understand
my brother-in-law's motivation. Maybe he thinks there are plenty of
coyotes, and those who live near our houses have settled into what
can be seen as a troubling pattern of pilfering the fruit under the pear
tree. Being this familiar with the yard can only end badly—either for
the coyote or for something else—a dog, or a neighbor's cat. So, if a

careless coyote were killed, the message would circulate to others that it's not a good idea to forage for fruit at four in the afternoon on the edge of a subdivision where men with guns live.

Maybe he thinks if this coyote were shot, the remaining wild coyotes in the floodplain would be more wary of humans, something that could only be a good thing in the expanding universe of eastern coyotes. At least this was what I projected of my brother-in-law's thoughts and what actions could come of them.

Most suburban yards are like little Fort Apaches, and mine is more like one of those French trading posts in the Canadian interior. My neighbors worry about getting too friendly with the natives outside the stockade, but I'm ready to invite them in because I imagine they have something I want: in this case, a sense of nearby wildness maintained in a place mostly settled and predictable.

And what would I trade for this opportunity? A little security for the neighborhood, maybe? I know my neighbors have cats. I know I put pets in jeopardy by inviting these predators close by. It's a chance I'm willing to take. Maybe I'm wrong, but for me the conflict is mostly about ownership, boundaries, borders between wild and domestic, yards, fields, and woods, territories, settlement and the outback, what's rightly ours and what's theirs. In my mind these boundaries aren't quite as clean as maybe they are for others. For most who live in the suburbs the boundaries are distinct and the coyotes have crossed them, and suburbanites are willing to defend their territory with a rifle and rely on the certainty of boundaries to underpin their own species' space.

I know as humans in our minds we are always building stockades, making distinctions, deciding what to allow inside and what to exclude, and this disagreement about where the fence should be between foraging coyotes and us is just another example. I should just drop it. I should withdraw back to my trading post and continue to offer up my salt block, occasional corn, and birdseed for the squirrels, deer, and raccoons. In exchange for food they trade me a fleeting glimpse, an image for a story or poem. I don't even own a gun. My boundaries are defended only with a porous split-rail fence, and my "wildlife refuge" sign tells the world I provide sanctuary for wild things.

I know what many readers will think, that I'm a coyote hugger with no common sense about country things or nature. I'm too sentimental and I imagine the woods are filled with Bambi. But I want somehow to put that to rest here. I know what wildness is. I've seen it. I know its cornerstone is death and struggle. Hobbes overstated the brutish and nasty nature of contemporary human lives, but I know what can go down out there in the woods. In the months before the pears ripen, I know that coyote stomachs are disproportionally filled with fawns. Even in our suburban woods these same pear-eating coyotes stalk and ambush when they can. These coyotes aren't cartoon characters like Wile E. Coyote with his oversized ears and duck-footed stance. These wild coyotes feast on newborn deer when they can, and cats if the neighborhood deer aren't available. They do what they need to to survive. They lick the blood from fallen oak leaves. When the deer are fawning, coyote scat contains nearly hardened tiny hooves instead of pear seeds.

This boundary conflict has sometimes taken a literary turn. As Barbara Kingsolver's novel *Prodigal Summer* opens, Deanna Wolfe, a young wildlife researcher in a Kentucky national forest, follows an animal trail uphill. A hard rain has just passed. She is frustrated, following the muddy trail of an animal she can't quite identify. The young solitary woman climbs upward through rhododendron, ascending into the dark old-growth forest. As she looks for tracks, Deanna thinks, "It was the size of a German shepherd, but no house pet. . . . The dog that had laid this trail, if dog it was, would have to be a wild and hungry one to be out in such a rain."

Instead of the prey she seeks, Deanna stumbles upon Eddie Bondo, an outsider with a rifle roaming after his own prey deep in the woods where she does her research. Deanna is at first put off by the hunter but is soon drawn to the mysterious man in the forest just as she is drawn to the tracks of the unseen animal, and she runs into Eddie Bondo several more times as she tries to solve her mystery. Eddie walks with Deanna as she follows her tracks in the forest and they talk, revealing a little more about why they are both in the woods. Eddie is interested in the forest, but he is also attracted to this young woman so deeply imbedded in the natural world. After talking for a while Bondo finally asks, "What's your game, lady?"

"Coyotes," Deanna admits, adding, "And bobcats, and bear, and fox," quickly obscuring her single interest in this creature.

"Why the carnivores?"

"No reason," she lies.

"I see. You're just partial. There's birdwatchers, and butterfly collectors, and there's gals like you that like to watch meat eaters."

Deanna senses his condescension and decides to explain: "They're the top of the food chain, that's the reason. . . . If they're good, then their prey is good, and its food is good. If not, then something's missing from the chain."

When *Prodigal Summer* was published in 2000, novelist/biologist Kingsolver anticipated the success of the coyote in the South through a plot and a series of compelling characters. She also, through Deanna and Eddie, articulated the primary question that has led me into this book: Is it a good thing to have a predator, a "carnivore," back at the top of the food chain? Should we celebrate, like Deanna, the coming of the coyote to our nearby forests, fields, and neighborhood yards, or like Eddie try to stop the advance in its tracks?

In *Prodigal Summer* we find out soon enough that Eddie Bondo has been drawn to the eastern mountains because of predation on sheep and cattle by coyotes, newly established in the East. He brings with him a deep, almost religious hatred of predators. Deanna, on the other hand, is a biologist who sees the good fortune of being in the right place at the right time: "What she had here on the mountain was a chance that would never come again for anybody: the return of a significant canid predator and the reordering of species it might bring about."

Deanna is not mushy-brained about it. She realizes she cannot predict what the return of coyotes will mean to the region. They could be pests. But she believes that coyotes are succeeding because "they were sliding quietly into the niche vacated two hundred years ago by the red wolf. . . . The ghost of a creature long extinct was coming in on silent footprints, returning to a place it had once held in the complex autonomy of this forest like a beating heart returned to its body."

Later, on another walk, Deanne and Eddie come to a clearing where from an overlook they can look down into Zebulon Valley.

"Sheep farms down there," Eddie says.

Deanna keeps her thoughts to herself, though internally she reflects on the coyote family recently discovered by the dairy farmer in the valley who found a den in a pasture edge and how he claimed to have wiped them out. "She didn't believe it . . . she knew a coyote family to be a nearly immortal creation. . . . 'Mother and father' was the farmer's appraisal of something beyond his ken; a coyote family was mostly females, sisters led by an alpha female, all bent on one member's reproduction."

I remembered this scene when I first heard of my brother-in-law's dilemma and of the pear tree across the creek where ripe fruit clutters the ground. Yellow jackets, drunk on the syrupy sweetness, buzz in the rotting pears collapsed and gone mealy in the late summer heat.

The coyotes in my brother-in-law's yard eating pears don't surprise me. The incident confirms for me what I've already read. Coyotes are not finicky eaters, says Jim Byford, professor and dean of the College of Agriculture and Applied Sciences at the University of Tennessee–Martin, in an article about coyote foodways for the newsletter *Southeast Farm Press* in 2004. Byford cites studies from all over the South—Mississippi, Tennessee, Alabama, Georgia, Florida, South Carolina, and Virginia—to show how when given the opportunity, coyotes will dine on deer, rabbits, snakes, lizards, possums, shrews, groundhogs, crayfish, beavers, raccoons, skunks, squirrels, grasshoppers, and beetles. "They'll eat about anything," Byford says, "as long as it will hold still long enough for them to grab it."

Byford admits coyotes also raid unsecured livestock, eating calves, goats, hogs, chickens, eggs, and even farm-raised catfish, but he wonders how often the coyotes merely clean up after kills left behind by wild dogs. "I'm sure the coyotes eat their fill once they find the remains—they're good at finding remains."

So, to call coyotes merely predators, as Eddie Bondo does, is a misstatement. As I've seen on many previous trips, coyotes are also scavengers. They don't always kill their food. They sometimes find it already dead or dying—and then they chase off the buzzards and finish off the food chain with a burp. Stories are common of hunters shooting a deer and tracking the animal down a blood trail for a half-hour and then finding a few choice bites missing from the carcass, or leaving a gut pile one day and coming back the next only to find the pile missing, probably a surprise smorgasbord on the overnight route of a foraging coyote pair. And yes, being opportunistic eaters, they will also kill and eat small domestic dogs and cats, "You know, the well-fed pampered kind," jokes Jim Byford.

Byford doesn't worry about coyote wiping anything out: "If there were an abundance of quail or rabbits, no doubt, they would eat some. But long before they ate enough to be of concern, they would switch to something easier to find or catch—like cotton rats or meadow mice."

When not filling their hungry bellies with meat, coyotes will also consume lots of wild fruit and plants—smilax berries, blackberries, blueberries, plums, persimmons, grass, acorns. They love persimmons, often the most common plant matter in coyote scats all through the fall, as evident by the shiny brown seeds.

If the season's right and the crops abound, they will also glean what domestic crops they can find—watermelons, corn, peaches, soybeans, even commercial stock feed. Farm to Table is a value coyotes have always known.

I too am an omnivore. I am seasonally omnivorous too, an opportunistic feeder, Publix to Fresh Market through the week, the local farmers' market on Saturday. If I am to remain a healthy *Homo sapiens*, I need a diversified diet. I share this trait with the coyotes under the pear tree.

Several weeks later my brother-in-law called and said the two healthy coyotes had come back for more pears. It could have been the two from the first day, or it could have been two others. He said he'd probably take a shot if he could get one. But now he has driven his family to the beach. "Every day between four and five they come by," he said. "Go over and see if you can spot them."

So I drove over late in the afternoon to look for our local coyotes, now clearly back in the floodplain after a year's absence. I say absence based on the silence. There had been a full calendar year without the chorus of howls and yips we had become accustomed to hearing. I'd assumed the owner of the floodplain, a man who uses the 250 acres for deer hunting, either trapped or shot them all out, but that was before I'd visited with John Kilgo and seen how hard it is to eradicate them. I knew every coyote trapped or shot from a tree stand is like spitting in the ocean. Every night I didn't hear them, I kept repeating Kingsolver's character's assertion of "a coyote family to be a nearly immortal creation."

You could say that over the last year I've developed faith in coyotes, their ability to survive, to thrive in the face of hate and the cunning of humans. They flourish when people try to kill them. They breed, den, raise their young, and populate their territories in spite of rampant mange, occasional rabies, persistent heartworms, illegal poison, trailing hounds, traps, rifles, speeding cars. They eat whatever they can find, and find almost everything there is to eat.

Another friend who lives in a subdivision near the pear tree texted to say he had seen a pair of coyotes in his neighborhood on two separate occasions, and then Mike Willis reported how his son was working inventory the night before up at Ingles (on the ridge about a mile from our house) and stepped out for some air about 2 a.m. and heard a cat meowing on one side of the building, and so he walked over and listened. The noise stopped in mid-meow, and out of the shadows walked a coyote with the cat hanging dead from its mouth. I started thinking about the story. Why is it that most would see that little act of predation as some sort of tragedy, and yet they wouldn't see the cat killing a songbird as tragic?

The same week my brother-in-law saw the coyotes foraging under the pear tree, another friend across town who owns a farm had been photographing an entire family group near a den site. He became acquainted with these rural coyotes when they too had been seen eating pears. He's not a hunter and did not feel any need to shoot them, except with a long lens and motor drive. The series of photos, maybe thirty images, are stunning. They show a complex narrative of coyote home life. When I first put them on a slide show, I wanted to score the bucolic cavalcade of images like a Disney film.

In one frame there are at least seven coyotes, three adults and four pups, spread through the field. Two of the pups are jet black, suggesting as I've read the recessive gene found in southern coyotes picked up somewhere along the species' genetic journey. In another frame two of the adults greet each other nose to nose, and one more walks into the image from stage right.

The adult coyote on the edge of the field is crouching. One click of the mouse on the program's magnifying glass reveals that this coyote is bending forward, as if it is recoiling from a pounce. More magnification shows it has something in its mouth. I zoom in even more, and it's clear the adult is returning to the family with a real mouse, a meal, not a tool, a dinner on Spartanburg's west side.

John Berger's classic essay "Why Look at Animals?" from his collection of essays *About Looking* points out that before the industrial revolution animals were with us in the center of our world and not pushed to the periphery of the circle of life. We needed them directly for food, energy, transportation, and clothing. Yet, he says, to believe that animals first entered our human imaginations as meat or leather is entirely a product of the nineteenth-century imagination: "The domestication of cattle did not begin as a simple prospect for milk and meat. Cattle had magical functions, sometimes oracular, sometimes sacrificial," or as Claude Levi-Strauss said in *The Savage Mind*, we were once married to animals.

My friend's photos show clearly what most people once knew. The connections between humans and animals can be intimate and relational. These relationships don't always go well. The eyes of an animal, Berger points out, are both attentive and wary.

But what of the relationship granted me to the wild world by my friend Julian's images? In the failure of seeing real coyotes at my brother-in-law's house, I scan the color photos one more time, dominated by the green and rich gold of late summer. Sometimes at least one coyote looks toward the camera, and in that glance I see Berger's attention and wariness. And who would blame the beast? The field and tree line harbors the den within sight of a country road, and I'm sure that there is more than one rural resident passing daily who would pull his gun from behind the pickup seat and blast away. Not many people in Spartanburg County, South Carolina, are firing off a camera shutter when face-to-face with coyotes.

Then Mike Willis showed me a series of photographs he'd downloaded on his iPad, taken with a game camera on the hunting lease he maintains a few miles below our house. I was surprised and hopeful. In the photos I could clearly see a crippled adult coyote, its forefoot atrophied from an old wound, pulling at a dead beaver carcass Mike had left out. The coyote was a lactating female. There was no way to prove it, but I believed it was the same coyote my brother-in-law had seen a year earlier foraging for pears under his tree. If so, she was at least three years old, so she had beaten the odds and somehow survived all of John Kilgo's graphs of the SRS coyotes and aged into the coyote 1 percent.

One photo taken by my west-side friend shows a coyote sentinel sitting atop one of five circular hay bales on the back edge of the field. His large ears—I say "him" as it is a big cinnamon and brown dog like I'd expect an alpha male to look—are laid back slightly, showing Berger's wariness. Maybe the animal hears the motor drive clicking in the distance.

Island Coyote

Of the amazing, innocent, all-sufficing beauty and
beneficence of nature, I feel that wild creatures must
be fully aware. At least I envy them their apparent utter
contentment—and this in the face of imminent and deadly
peril.—Archibald Rutledge, "Why I Envy Wild Things"

On the ferry ride to Cat Island and the Tom Yawkey Wildlife
Center near Georgetown, South Carolina, I heard my first (but not
my last) story of a dead island coyote. On the short ride across the
Intercoastal Waterway in a state pontoon boat I asked Dennis, the
dreadlocked boatman, if there were coyotes on the island, and if so,
what the resident experts knew about them.

"Oh, I know we got the coyotes," he said, smiling and showing a gold
tooth. "I'd like to know where the experts are." Then he told a story
of running over a coyote on the causeway to South Island almost a
decade before. He'd hit another one later, but killing what proved to be
the first South Island coyote was what Dennis choose to tell me about.

Seventy-nine-year-old retired Department of Natural Resources
wildlife biologist Phil Wilkinson sat beside me for the short boat ride.
Phil was my guide on this bright, warm February day. Between us was
propped a two-horsepower outboard Phil planned to use on a spare
boat for his continuing, long-term alligator research on the island.
Next to his foot was his ever-present camera bag. Phil might be as
good a photographer as he is a scientist. His photos have appeared
in magazines, galleries, and shows, and are displayed prominently on

the walls of the house where he lives in Georgetown. That the Yawkey Center is a place Phil knows intimately is obvious from his choice of subject matter for his photographs, from coastal scenes to wildlife, and he is still deeply connected to the place after fourteen years of retirement. His connection is both personal and professional. His research project still rates its own pickup parked across the water, and that's where we were headed.

Being "an alligator man," Phil wanted to show me his research sites—the slough called Cujo Gaul where there was a good chance to see Cujo and "Big Bertha," two of his storied animals. Riding down to Georgetown I'd thought my interest in alligators on this project as only peripheral. I'd forgotten that old axiom of the natural history trade, Aldo Leopold's web, how one thing is always hitched to another. As I had explained to Phil on the phone, my coyote project is a long way from a scientific study. I wanted to drive around the South for a year and listen to stories about coyotes and look for a few. Phil seemed intrigued with the expansion of coyotes into the South, and so when I'd told him about my plan to track the elusive new predator, he'd invited me down to Yawkey, a place where the fate of southern wildlife, new and old, is colliding.

Some speculate that Hurricane Hugo in 1989 contributed to the surge of coyotes on the coast. "The biggest blow up was after Hugo," one manager of a coastal reserve asserted. "Lots of damage to fox pens."

Phil thinks there may be some validity to the Hugo speculation. The deer population on Yawkey's South Island was artificially high before the storm. The herd had been fed for decades, and there was no hunting pressure, and Hugo would have been precoyote. In the 1980s there had been a paper by biologists about work on fawn predation on Cat Island. A portion of the Yawkey preserve had shown high percentages for fawn mortality. Of course, managing wildlife is always complex. At the height of the deer herd explosion in the 1980s, even though there were no coyotes to contend with, one study by wildlife biologist Mark Epstein on Cat and South Islands showed an extremely high radio collared fawn mortality rate—approaching 90 percent. What was killing all those fawns? Phil had his theories: "Big Bobcats, alligators, even red foxes." He said at night you could sit at the Yawkey Center and hear the bobcats making kills, and he'd had one instance where a big, radio-collared alligator had converged on a radio-collared fawn. And finally, "I'd photographed a fox den off and on and during fawning season, and there was always a fawn out front for the pups to gnaw on."

After Hugo the deer herd never recovered the way everybody thought it would. There were still food plots planted and the clover was left uneaten. There were no deer tracks around feeding stations. Phil suspects that deer learned feeding stations were ambush sites, especially for vulnerable fawns.

"It didn't occur to anybody to think about coyotes. Then about that time I saw new tracks and figured out whose they were."

Phil said he saw his first tracks of coyotes on North Island (the area of the Tom Yawkey Wildlife Center across Winyah Bay) in 1995 or 1996, and it was almost a decade before that first one was run down on the causeway between Cat Island and South Island. Between the arrival of the first pioneering coyotes and the present, the smart adaptive canids had played hell with the nesting turtles every June. Around 2000 a Warren Wilson College student working on the South Island beach during nesting season came to Phil and said a big bobcat or panther was eating the turtle eggs. "Well, I knew it wasn't likely a bobcat and definitely not a panther, so I went to look and saw the tracks of a pair of coyotes." They kept watching that summer and deduced it was a family group running the beach—two adults and their young.

The predation was difficult to control, and even before the arrival of coyotes, turtle nests had always been susceptible to egg robbing— sand crabs, raccoons, hogs, even locals. Turtle eggs were always in demand. As a boy Phil himself had hunted the same beaches for eggs and reports they are best boiled as they contain no albumen and so are hard to scramble. For a long time the efforts to control the coyotes were unsuccessful. "Raccoons could be trapped out, but with coyotes, you're talking about somebody."

It wasn't until several summers after the coyotes were first discovered feasting on eggs that the turtle team, through a combination of screening, patrol, and trapping, dropped the predation of the nests to a manageable level. Now, Phil said, DNR and researchers run an active trapping program in the spring before the turtles arrive, working to "knock back" the coyote population on the front beach.

Around the same time the coyotes started raiding the turtle nests, another thing got Phil's attention. He found one of his alligator study nests pilfered by coyotes, and after that, Phil began to take into account the changing calorie budget of the island's wildlife. Coyotes were taking their place at the table.

When the ferry docked on the other side of the water Dennis helped Phil off with his motor. We were met there by Tom Yawkey's resident biologist, Jamie Dozier, a good friend of Phil's and an observer of Yawkey's wildlife dramas since May of 2007. Jamie invited us into the small conference room of a building near the landing everyone calls the Ferry House, and we sat and talked there for an hour or so. Two posters filled the wall behind us and I was instantly interested in the research by Cady Etheredge and Trent Eschew, both Clemson University students. Cady Etheredge's work, "Coyotes and Raccoons and Loggerhead Sea Turtles on a S.C. Barrier Island," prompted the beginning of our discussion.

"I don't think coyotes and raccoons overlapped in their original ranges," Jamie offered.

"When coyotes showed up on the beach the raccoons stopped eating the turtle eggs," Phil added.

"Do they eat the hatchings too?" I asked, imaging the coyotes lined up waiting for the little turtles to crawl and gobbling them up like snack candy.

"There's a fairly low find-rate," Phil said. "But if they're walking the beach on the night they come out, they'll gobble them up."

"Cameras are big now in the wildlife field," Jamie said. "They're being used for things they've never been used for before. There is video of coyotes waiting patiently beside turtle nests for the mother to finish laying her eggs."

Asked about other predators Jamie explained that hogs are an issue, especially on North Island. "They're here on Cat Island and over on South Island but not out on the front beach."

Phil and Jamie talked about how hogs have been around hundreds years in the lowcountry, but it was only the last several decades that they'd become a problem. Why was that? Phil invoked his deep knowledge of the coastal hunting communities, "People in the past worked the hell out of them. If a damn pig put down a track somebody looking at it knew where the foot came from. In the old days they knew what they were doing hunting hogs. They had hog dogs."

"People still love to hunt them," Jamie added. "You can hunt them twelve months a year with no offseason."

I wanted to know what interested Jamie most about the coyotes on Yawkey and what his attitude was toward their control, so I asked him directly about the current situation.

"Coyotes are a species that everyone seems to revile," he said. "We've sat around here and talked about that. Coyotes and rattlesnakes, that's two species without many friends."

About that time two green pickups came roaring down the sand road and we all glanced out the window as they streaked past. I laughed to myself, and made a note in my journal. It was clear now how a coyote could get run over on a sand road.

We picked up our conversation again after the trucks had passed. I could tell Jamie had other work to do and I didn't want to hold him up. Did he worry about coyotes killing fawns?

"Even if they are whacking the deer in local spots, I have faith the deer will adapt," he said. "For ten thousand years the deer and red wolves lived together. Deer did alright back then."

He reminded me that the background for all he was saying was mostly speculation, since "we don't really know a great deal about coyotes in the South yet." But then he added, "You've got to have money to do research, and nobody wants to fund coyote research unless you are figuring out ways to kill them."

It was time to see the preserve, so I asked Jamie if he had any final thoughts, and he said, "Just that we're not going to get rid of all the coyotes here, and so we really don't care about them except that as they impact the endangered sea turtles. If they get the deer, they get the deer."

As we drove the straight main road across Cat Island toward South Island we passed a road grader. The driver raised an index finger toward us. "That's Steve, the heavy equipment driver," Phil said. "We'll track him down and talk to him later. He does most of the trapping on the island."

The long road through Cat Island's center was bordered by longleaf and loblolly pine. Phil filled me in on his life in the lowcountry as we cruised. He talked about how after growing up in a plantation house along the north bank of the Santee River, he did graduate work in wildlife at Auburn, and then in 1962 he returned home to manage a large plantation given to South Carolina's Department of Natural Resources upstream from Georgetown called Dirleton. The plantation on the Pee Dee River was designated by the donor to be developed for waterfowl hunting, and Phil was chosen by DNR to carry out the plan, which included restoring old rice fields so that they could be used as impoundments for managed waterfowl.

Phil spent three and a half years on Dirleton and then was transferred by the agency to South Island, where he was assigned to assist Mr. Tom Yawkey, the millionaire owner of the Boston Red Sox and twenty thousand coastal acres on the Winyah Bay. The extensive and wild Cat, South, and North Island properties had suffered from lack of management when Phil arrived, so Mr. Yawkey cut a deal with DNR for Phil to work as manager in return for the agency's access to the islands. Phil worked for Mr. Yawkey for ten years, until Yawkey's death in 1976, when the land passed to DNR in the Yawkey will and a ten-million-dollar trust was established for its management. From 1976 until the present the Yawkey property had served as a South Carolina Heritage Preserve and as the Tom Yawkey Wildlife Center, a reserve not open to the public, to be used for management, education, and research.

Phil began researching in earnest when Yawkey was added to the state reserve with all of its "endangered species, shore birds, pelicans, alligators, all sorts of stuff." He also did shorebird surveys down the coast at Cape Romaine for three years, three-day surveys twice a month.

Phil reminded me that the first phase of the red wolf recovery project had played out just down the coast from Yawkey. He did radio tracking of the collared wolves down there on Bull Island and was also invested in live trapping of raccoons on Drum Island in Charleston Harbor, because "at the time it was the largest white Ibis nesting colony anywhere, and raccoons were playing hell with it. We set aside January to totally focus on trapping Drum Island. For several years we live trapped between sixty-five and ninety raccoons each year on the island," and he said every one went to Bull Island to be used in the red wolf project—feeding wolves. That project went on for a good many years until recently, when the Bull Island wolves were moved up the coast to Alligator River.

As we talked, Phil remembered being on Bull Island once with nature photographer Tom Blagdon. They were standing together admiring a red-tailed hawk in a dead pine when Phil happened to look down in front of him, and standing there about twenty-five yards away was a male red wolf, looking straight at the two of them. "We fixed our gaze on him but he turned, leaped across a ditch and disappeared in the woods. For me, that was the highlight of our trip."

We drove for a while along the Cat Island canals, passing the managed waterfowl marshes and the open pine ridges. Dozens of alligators basked on the tidal mudflat, many with a notch cut out of their tails where Phil had trapped, marked, and released them in past years. As the gators slid into the sloughs a healthy flurry of hundreds of black-crowned night herons rose from the rush and helicoptered briefly in the air, and settled back from whence they came before the truck passed. This was one of those moments I'd been pining for all winter, an open window into a truly wild place, with forces well beyond my daily life. The night herons and alligators existed in a web of eternal tension, a prey–predator dance established by their genes eons ago. Yet there was an ease in which the birds moved among the black, basking behemoths. Sometimes they settled back within what looked like range of the jaws, and yet there was a calm that morning on the marsh. It was not feeding time, or maybe the alligators were too cold to care that the birds were playing tag.

Phil stopped to show me some of the old trunks (wooden water-control structures) built between the ponds. Today they are constructed of huge treated beams held together with galvanized bolts, but in the old days Phil explained they would have been sawed from abundant local rot-resistant cypress and fashioned with pegs. His familiarity with these structures was what made Mr. Yawkey partial to Phil working on his place in the 1960s.

Water control trunks are like fossils from a past life, solid structures developed long ago for which no better alternative has arisen. One of Phil's major life themes is the loss of old ways he grew up with, but here was an example of an old way that had survived, a design brought from West Africa to the lowcountry three hundred years ago that was used extensively in the rice fields of plantations like where Phil grew up, and a better alternative still can't be found today.

As Phil explained the trunks, I asked him about Archibald Rutledge, South Carolina's most famous plantation poet, a man whose reputation rests on his return in middle age to the island world he abandoned as a young man for a teaching job the Northeast. Rutledge won the John Burroughs Medal for his nature writing in 1930 and was the state's first poet laureate from 1934 until his death in 1973. Phil said Archie would often stop to pick him up hitching to school on the Charleston road, and so he knew his family's famous neighbor quite well. Rutledge and Phil are intertwined in my mind. Phil knows the Santee Delta with as deep a knowledge as men did back in Rutledge's generation. He's hunted and trapped there, and he's studied the wildlife with an eye toward longer complex patterns. I wondered what Archie would have thought about coyotes coming into the country he hunted, troubling "the woods and wild things" he loved. I asked Phil, but the question didn't seem to interest him much. Instead of answering he pointed out that besides water control, the trunks also acted as impromptu feeding stations for birds and even alligators. I watched as fish, large and small, congregated around the openings. The feeding fish broke the green surface, stippling the canal as they fed. Feeders, feeding upon feeders. There were signs the food chain extended in all directions everywhere. As Phil had said, now, even the coyotes were pushing up to the trough. I stood and wondered, watching the fish, whether life for a coyote was easier or harder in the South. They'd only had a few decades at most to learn their table manners, but did they know where the chow lines were shortest?

Calories, I imagined, were easier to come by on a barrier island than a midwestern prairie, or on the west Texas high plains. Researchers across the South have shown that coyotes in all seasons eat animals mostly, but that vegetation occurs in high frequency all year as well. They use roadways as corridors and eat roadkill found there, and insects are eaten when they are available. Variability is the constant, as John Kilgo had shown. Whenever the fawns drop, the coyotes eat fawns. They eat what they can find. All over the

South they eat wild fruit when it's ripe—"opportunistic omnivores," they are classified.

We drove on and passed a small borrow pit in the pines where Phil said they'd caught, tagged, and worked up two big gators. Phil pointed to a large basking alligator on the far bank. "That's Cujo over there," he said, and explained the gator's name came from a nearby body of water where he was first caught. The spot was called Cujo Gaul, and island legend said a black man named Cujo once drowned there.

Adding a nice footnote to my gastronomical reflections about island food budgets, we drove down a long canal called West Cleveland Lodge, stirring up a storm of wading great egrets and herons. We were near the site of Grover Cleveland's hunting lodge (destroyed in a marsh fire in the 1920s) where he once hunted ducks, but where now Big Bertha, a female alligator almost as old as Phil, resided, hunting and eating a duck or two herself. "She's still nesting. She skipped last year, but nested in 2011." He asks me to roll down the window and said to the old lady, "Hello, Bertha."

After showing me his alligators and the trunks, Phil wove back to the main road and soon we were on the long causeway to South Island. The marshes managed by the state for game birds crowded both sides of the truck, and as we bumped along at a fast clip I imagined the first Yawkey roadkill coyote trotting on the narrow spit of sand and gravel as a speeding DNR pickup overtook it and there was no place to go but under the wheels.

Once we'd crossed the causeway, Phil stopped to see if Steve was at home. Tucked in the pines were several garages, a maintenance shop, a dozen tractors, the yellow road grader we'd seen Steve on earlier, a bulldozer, and a fleet of pickups, some running, some not. There were boats and trailers. Phil hoped to attach the two-horse engine he'd brought over to one of them and cruise the sloughs for his alligator research. All the big machines triggered a reflection of the place in an earlier time. Phil explained how different management of the wildlife center was back then. On Mr. Yawkey's place in the 1960s they still did things the way they had been done forever—mostly by hand with a large crew. They figured things out. They constantly adapted and adapted again. They couldn't do things the way they do them today with big machines. They couldn't overpower island problems. "Fixing things, maintaining things, was like an art. Change took a long time. Everybody on my crew understood this well. They understood it much better than a goddamn CEO," Phil said. "So much is being lost. Today I don't think they lie awake at night figuring out how to get over the hump."

Sometimes Phil sounded like an old man pining for "the good old days," and other times an objective scientist ready to stride into the next research window. Phil's both and neither. He was seventy-nine but he had his feet firmly planted in the present. He sends me e-mails and takes photos of the marsh with a fancy new digital camera, even though he has successfully resisted getting a cell phone.

Phil stopped at his research project's "gear locker," a small room in Mr. Yawkey's old garage. We hauled in the little two-horse engine and he propped it among the nets and nooses. Seemed nobody locked anything, so Phil simply pulled the door shut. Then we walked over to see the coyote head Jamie had mentioned earlier. The first island coyote casualty was mounted with its mouth gapping wide, staring glass-eyed from a cypress-paneled wall of what's known on South Island as the Den, a two-hundred-year-old hall moved there by Mr. Yawkey to serve as just that, an area to relax in when he and his wife were visiting. The Yawkey house burned in the 1950s, and rather than build back a sea island mansion again, the wealthy couple had stayed in separate trailers on their visits.

The coyote head on the wall kept company for eternity with a stuffed bobcat, a black bear, a plump beaver caught forever chewing on a stump like a lollipop, and a hundred sets of buck antlers. I looked into the coyote's glass eyes and hoped for some reflection of Aldo

Leopold's "fierce green fire," but I saw nothing there but the costume jewelry glint of two taxidermists' glass beads. The little gold plaque on the wooden mount said simply "First Coyote Yawkey Wildlife Center March 8, 2005."

Phil saw Steve's truck was home, so he figured he was eating lunch, and so he went to the door to tell Steve we were going to the beach to look for coyote tracks. We'd be back to talk to him later in the afternoon.

Once Phil was in the truck and driving I used the hook of "old ways vanished" to get him to swerve back toward the subject of island coyotes by mentioning an article that's come out about an issue just up the coast at a wealthy enclave called DeBordieu. The article outlined a familiar skirmish among southerners who want what they see as an invading army of coyotes trapped, and those who don't. The article had explained how hired nuisance trappers have ringed DeBordieu's perimeter with sets of traps to try to catch and remove the coyotes. It was not clear whether the coyotes had just been observed or whether they had killed pets, but the way the situation was described made it sound as if they were protecting a firebase in Vietnam or defending against attacking Indians.

This idea both amused and infuriated Phil, who grew up on the north bank of the Santee in the country among wild things, just downstream from where Rutledge had written about his similar relationship with "woods and wild things" in best-selling prose and poetry. In *Home by the River*, Rutledge writes of returning to his family plantation Hampton after fifty-six-years' absence, and the poet says of the Santee Delta that it is a place where "one comes upon the allurement of beauty's reticence and shadowy avoidance, the haunting charm of the inaccessible." Being a part of this reticent and inaccessible world was one of the old ways Phil can't abandon. Human life to him is still a strand in a mesh of wildness, and we live—if we live well—on and within that web, not apart from it. We do not ring the perimeter with traps to keep us safe. "These folks up there with all their money feel like if they get together they can have life the way they want it—with the coyotes and the sand washing away and all that stuff. If they don't like coyotes around or their beach receding, they better move," Phil said.

Phil was not suggesting he knows coyotes in the intimate and specific data-driven way he knows alligators, but he does feel he has an intuition about wild things that gives him the capital to speculate on their future: coyotes, they're newcomers, so their role and impact on island ecosystems isn't even settled yet; they're here to stay; and they will probably be very successful at filling the niche vacated when red wolves were eradicated from the coast hundreds of years ago.

The sand road out to the beach made a turn through a bank of shrubs, and Phil pointed out the two-track bisected what everyone called "the bone yard," a place where if some animal was found dead on the preserve (or hit by a speeding pickup) the carcass was brought back and tossed here. I asked Phil to stop, and we stepped out into this field of bones and scraps of flesh, dried and rotting. The ground was littered with various skulls like a macabre nature exhibit. I identified deer, several raccoons, four or five alligators, two pigs, an armadillo, and some sort of dark bird. I didn't see anything resembling the long snout of a canid.

I was uncomfortable in the spot. Phil didn't like the bone yard either. Our brief visit prompted him to remember, "When I was a kid you shot something and got it ready for the table."

The lack of coyote carcasses drying in the sun suggested that they dined elsewhere, at the beach's sushi bar or in the upland's butchery, habitats that offered plenty of healthy alternatives to that spread of carrion.

A little further on Phil parked his pickup where the sand road climbed over the secondary line of dunes. When we stepped out he saw right away there were animal tracks headed, like us, toward the beach. The first tracks showed Phil there had been two bobcats only hours before, one large and one small, following a big deer. The deer tracks were the familiar twin crescents. The bobcat tracks, a set of pads with round circles but no claws, and they were not yet filled with blowing sand.

About halfway out to the beach Phil spotted what I was looking for, two sets of canid tracks in the sand ruts, more pointed than domestic dogs, with oblong pads and pricks of sand where the claws had dug in. We followed, and Phil noted how they seemed to have paused and drifted closer together on the rim of the last dune, maybe taking in the ocean view. Then the pair continued down onto the beach and took off, running, swerving back and forth, coming together, hurtling apart like children let loose at the ocean the first time. They ran for twenty yards and then climbed the dune and dispersed into the interdune scrub.

I was as excited as they had been. We'd stumbled onto this frozen coyote moment before the rising tide had erased it forever. We'd seen the evidence of their private lives and followed them for a brief moment. But I was also conflicted, for this is the very beach where the huge prehistoric sea turtles lumber ashore each year to dig their nests from the same sand, as they have done for eons, and the turtle nesting coincides with the denning of the island coyotes. In the late spring there would be coyote parents hunting this beach for protein to feed their hungry pups back in their dens. Did I have to make a choice as to who to pull for? Couldn't I just forget the conservation conflicts and enjoy the beach for an afternoon?

As much as I was pulling for the coyotes, I knew it was impossible to forget the conflicts with sea turtles, and how the turtles had the better hand: a designation as an endangered species. "For most of the wild things on earth the future must depend upon the conscious of mankind," Archie Carr had written about his hope for these ancient creatures. "It is not too late to ensure a future for the sea turtle."

We followed the coyote tracks to where they left the beach and sat there with our backs to the sharp dune escarpment and ate our sandwiches, calorie loading for the afternoon. I watched a pod of dolphins feeding along the lonely coast. Five fins surfaced in a regular pattern as they foraged for the running fish. We didn't have to search far and wide for food like a turtle, dolphin, or coyote. We had sandwiches of factory ham and industrial cheese and a Big Agriculture apple. The lunch was good in the way that all food consumed out in the open is good.

Sitting there munching my apple in silence gave me the time to get sentimental about the coyote pair frolicking on the deserted beach. Was it an amorous couple? I knew from my reading that mid-February was probably near the end of the breeding season. Could these two sets of tracks gyrating apart and together be the signs of bonding? Did a male lead his mate out to the beach for a quick session of court and spark?

Or was it a mother and a yearling pup, two aunts, cousins, brothers, sisters? If they were out together I imagined they were probably part of an extended family, and this morning or midday trip to the beach was part of family life. There was no way for me to know any of this for sure, but it was fun to speculate about and weave into my own story of coyotes in the South.

I did not articulate these thoughts out loud. I don't imagine Phil would have been sentimental about either coyotes or sea turtles. I don't think he's sentimental about death. He knows "All Things Must Pass," as George Harrison famously sang, and that the cold hand of the reaper will come to pass over everyone and every living thing. He's also a wildlife biologist with deep experience of the waxing and waning of the creation, and so he knows that the death of a species is a lot more significant than the death of an individual within that group, and so his sentiments probably lie, when he has them, with the survival of threatened turtles over populations of flourishing island coyotes in the first flush of their colonizing.

And me? I finished my ham sandwich and looked out at what is called by poets "the timeless sea," and yet the coyote tracks pointed to a problem tied closely to the very real present. I'd spent most of my life with my environmentalist sympathies building constantly for the sea turtles. After all, they've been in the big-budget ad campaigns that come with being cute in a reptilian sort of way. Protecting their nests had become a vacation activity on southern barrier islands. There were even children's books about them nesting. All that was good, and it has helped raise the awareness of the plight of this ancient and powerful creature, but it had not stopped the carnage. Was it really the coyotes that were keeping the sea turtles on the worldwide list of the most concern? Isn't it really industrial fishing and coastal real estate agents who should be taking the blame and leading the charge to stop the killing? If we regulated these industries as they should be, wouldn't there be plenty of protein to go around?

I was glad that everyone was doing everything possible to give the turtles a fighting chance, including "knocking back" the coyotes that had learned how to purchase a quick raw omelet on the beachfront. What I didn't want, though, was for folks to lose sight of the beauty of the mating predators dancing on the beach. I wanted folks to stop hating the coyotes, and instead to see them as part and parcel now of this scene. The reintroduction of the red wolves might have failed down the coast at Bull Island, but here on South Island the coyotes had found their way, and they were settled in.

We stopped by the maintenance shop again to see if Steve was back. Though there were four green DNR trucks out front, there was no Steve, so we headed back toward Cat Island, down the long sand causeway where the first coyote had been hit and killed. As we drove, Phil pointed out a sweep of marsh to our left with a single jutting palmetto in the distance. He said he'd photographed that spot in the past and made a striking print from the image with the title *One Tree Marsh*. Phil slowed down and I tried to take a picture out the window with my phone camera, but being no photographer, all I got was two disappointing overexposed horizontal bars of color, a base band of black where the stunning charcoal winter marsh should have been, and a band of washed out blue for the unforgettable azure lowcountry sky.

When we were back up to speed on the causeway, we saw a pickup coming at us, driving on the wrong side of the road. Phil reversed lanes, but didn't seem concerned, switching from right to left on the narrow road bounded on both sides by marsh. The truck approached at a good clip. As it came closer we saw that the pickup dragged a flat rake and large section of chain to smooth out the road's surface. The contraption made an awful racket as it bumped to a stop. Phil pulled up window to window with the other vehicle. "Hello, Steve," Phil said and the man in the driver's seat nodded.

As we talked another green pickup drew close from the direction of the mainland, slipped past us, and then quickly picked up speed again down the causeway. There was a man in a DNR uniform in the cab of the second truck and two men in street clothes sitting in the bed. The two in the bed had red bandanas wrapped around their heads to keep the winter sun off. "Who is that?" Phil asked.

"That's the crew marking woodpecker trees," Steve said.

"You have any time to talk with this man about coyotes?" Phil asked.

"Come on back to the shop," Steve answered.

"We'll drive down to turn around, then head back."

"Why don't you just back up? It's just half a mile." Steve joked, and accelerated, pulling the rattling rake.

The woodpecker crew had headed for the shop as well, and the three of them were out of the truck and milling around by the time we pulled up. You could tell it was getting late in the day, a Friday, and most of the serious work checking red-cockaded woodpecker trees was done for the week. The two bandanas in the woodpecker crew asked Steve if there was anything else to do. "Go on out and open up those four hog traps," Steve instructed the two young guys who had been riding in the back of the pickup. "I won't be around to check them this weekend."

Phil asked about the surface-smoothing equipment Steve was pulling behind the pickup, and Steve spoke proudly of his jerry-rigged contraption. He'd tried dragging a piece of chain-link fence, but small shards of wire kept breaking off and puncturing the truck tires, so he went with the flat rake and a big tow chain instead. "It works just fine."

I was worried about taking Steve's time on a dwindling Friday afternoon, but he seemed willing to linger and talk, so we headed into the big shop through one of two sets of double garage doors. I looked around. The space was filled with power tools, bins of nails, clamps, PVC pipe joints for fitting plumbing, and lots of planks and beams. There were even guns propped on some of the workbenches and I was reminded for a moment of what it must be like on a firebase where insurgents might overrun the perimeter at any moment. There were plenty of the remnants of former firefights with wildlife. There were dozens of buck skulls along the walls. But this was a working shop and not a hunting lodge, so on the concrete floor on one side there was a trunk under construction for water control in the reserve's ponds. Two huge treated pine beams were parallel and up on their edges. The agency's construction crew had not added any of the cross pieces yet, and it had not taken on the distinctive "H" (with a long cross piece) shape of the rice field trunks we'd seen earlier.

Steve had been hired to run the heavy equipment, but his job now seemed to be to act as a sort of island foreman, coordinating all the various maintenance projects. I could see just from what was around the shop that he was as essential to this place as the tides. I could see that working on the refuge was full of everyday engineering problems like smoothing the bumpy causeway road, or controlling the water in the ponds; some of the tasks were simple and others were quite complex daily conundrums that if left untended would allow the island to quickly revert to a wilder, unmanaged state Mr. Yawkey's millions had come a long way toward holding back.

I imagined folks like Steve and the turtle researchers saw the coyotes as just another problem to be solved as cheaply and efficiently as possible. Others, like Phil and Jamie, took positions that seemed a little more philosophical with longer natural payoffs (the balance over the long run of the prey–predator game). I thought they would probably all agree, though, that every environmental solution is a short-term fix on some scale: the road gets bumpy again, and the trunks rot in the semitropical heat and moisture, and the coyotes breed successfully again on the beachfront.

Inside, Steve showed Phil and me the huge skull of an alligator over thirteen feet long they'd found dead. "Died of heat, or sun. Crawled up on the beach and just got too hot." Steve explained. The skull was shaped like a huge shovel blade and was clean of all flesh. Steve and Phil debated how to clean the skull even more so that it could be displayed up in the Ferry House. "We can bleach it, or paint it white," Steve said. Phil voted for bleach. "If you paint it, it will always look painted," he said.

Then I noticed a string of coyote tails hanging next to a workbench. Five tails dangled from a nail. I asked Steve how they've been caught and he said each was from an animal he'd trapped the season before. "I'll be glad to show you the traps," he said.

The gray and fluffy tails had black tips, as if each, as Sean Poppy had pointed out about Scooter's tail, had been dipped one by one in a can of paint. I'd not yet been within touching distance of any part, living or dead, of a southern coyote in my project. I'd heard the coyotes howl and I'd seen their tracks and scat, and I'd passed at high speed a few dead ones on the side of the interstate. I'd seen two living animals briefly behind our house, and I'd stood with Scooter in his pen, but I'd never touched the coat of a coyote, so I reached up and stroked the string of tails and I was surprised at how soft they were, how much they'd give way to the passing of my hand over them and through their fur. Researchers had told me coyotes are often submissive when they are caught in the traps, and with some of them, if you have the nerve, you can walk right up and grab them behind the neck.

Steve didn't give me the details of their lives or deaths, but I imagined these five coyotes had been hunting the island the year before. They'd played on the beach like the two loping individuals whose tracks we'd followed at lunch, and yes, in season they'd maybe eaten, or planned to eat, some endangered turtle eggs, just like Phil had done sixty years before from the very same beach. Maybe they were a single family group, related, a clan of cousins and uncles and aunts, ten or fifteen generations after migration east, now making a living like pilgrims on a foreign shore in the island's spartina and black rush and palmetto. I doubted they were tourists, though like tourists, they had developed a serious appetite for seafood. I expect that before they were trapped and dispatched they knew their way around. They had their habits and routines to maintain, like Steve did, dragging the causeway road. They knew what to fear and what to prize. Sometimes one of them screwed up, and ended up under the wheels of a pickup or in a trap.

"Let's sit for a minute," Phil said, and Steve pulled over an old office chair on rollers. Phil and I sat on a blue vinyl van seat, like locals on the front porch of a country shack, and we three talked for ten minutes about the island coyotes.

Steve was knowledgeable and opinionated. I started the conversation by asking when he'd first seen the island coyotes and where. He said he'd been seeing them on the island since 1995 or 1996, often on or near what they all call the Goose Pond, an area of marsh up the causeway. "They took a toll on things," he added. "We used to have deer, turkey, and coons. Now I like to say all we have is bobcats, coyotes, and hogs."

How about the agency's trapping program on Yawkey? He said he'd be getting back into that in the next few months as the turtle-nesting season approached. "I had no problem with the coyotes until they started digging up the turtle eggs," he said. He added they try to knock them back every year on the beachfront so the nests will have a chance. He admitted it's an uphill battle. "They're new here. In five to eight more years, they'll be adapted like everything else, and they'll be harder to get."

We'd been talking fifteen minutes and the men were back from checking the traps Steve had sent them off to open. I could tell everybody was getting a little antsy to get back to the dwindling routines of a Friday afternoon, so I stood up and Phil took my lead.

"I'd like to see your traps before we go," I said, taking Steve up on his offer to show me his wares. Steve led Phil and me to the back corner to an old shopping cart filled with number 2 foothold traps, chains, and trap stakes. This trapper's lair was nothing like Cormac McCarthy trapper's cabin in *The Crossing*. There was no secret council with the spirits of the animals, little deep accumulated wisdom of the trappers who had come before, no magician's chamber, and certainly no "basilica dedicated to a practice soon to be extinct to the trades of men." This trapping operation was part of the day-to-day work of a shop full of greasy tools and dusty parts, some metal, some bone.

Steve picked up one of the traps and explained how there was a gap when the jaws snap shut so that the animal's leg could have a little play, and how the jaws were coated with plastic to pad them. If the animal was caught it couldn't pull out, but the pressure of the release of the coil springs wasn't great enough to snap the leg or even, many times, break the skin. He pointed out the swivel on the chain so when the trapped animal panicked it could pirouette or jerk against the trap and not get tangled up.

Then Steve forced the trap open and engaged the levers, revealing the pan. He tried to trigger it as a coyote would in the field to show me the action, but it would not close. He handed the malfunctioning trap over to one of the bandana guys watching from the periphery and told him to fix it, then popped open another one and placed his fingers inside and eased the trap closed on three fingers of his right hand. He let the greasy black trap dangle from his pinched fingers and after he'd made his point, he acted like he was trying unsuccessfully to extract himself, but couldn't. "Get me out of this thing," he joked to those of us watching.

Danny's Field

If I hadn'a believed it, I wouldn'a seen it.

—Attributed to Mark Twain

Larry Stallings took us out to Danny's Field in Auburn University's Solon Dixon Forestry Education Center's white Ford pickup. It was early in March and the morning sun rose straight ahead as we drove north on Route 29 in "L.A." (Lower Alabama), forty miles from the Gulf of Mexico. We sat three abreast on the single bench seat and Larry narrated in his dry, flat Alabama drawl. Mike Willis sat in the middle with his hand cupped over his ear so he could hear what Larry was saying. I leaned into the passenger-side door taking notes. We passed Alabama forests and fields alternating in sections along the country road. "Most time you see 'em in the fields," Larry said. "I keep a rifle in the truck for hogs and coyotes. Most time it's just one. If you see two it's usually a male and a female."

Mike and I were down from South Carolina for a week touring Solon Dixon to scare up whatever we could learn about Alabama coyotes. We were there as guests of Rhett Johnson, the retired director of the Solon Dixon Forestry Center. I'd met Rhett in Spartanburg, where he lectured about longleaf pine ecosystems, and when he heard I was interested in coyotes, he invited me down to Alabama. He said he'd set me up with a place to stay at the center and take me out and to see the property. Mike Willis had a week off and wanted to tag along.

I'll admit that when I first heard from Rhett that Auburn University has 5,300 acres of pine, hardwood, and river bottom swamp, I imagined that I might have finally hit on an eastern coyote Shangri-la. I thought the forest center might be a perfect refuge for the pioneering wild southern canines. I thought all that land might offer a spot where coyotes could live out their lives like predators on the wild plains of Africa, performing daily in a sort of blood drama produced by Walt Disney, some place like James Dickey's "The Heaven of Animals," where the wild prey and predators live "at the cycle's center," and where they could let "their instincts / wholly bloom."

But on arrival I learned from Rhett that the work that goes on at Solon Dixon is much more complex than my cartoon wilderness tableau. At Solon Dixon the "cycle's center" is managed with particular objectives in mind, and it has been managed that way for thirty years since the Dixon family gifted the former cutover timber plantation (at its time the largest gift ever by a living donor) to Auburn University.

The management objectives of the Solon Dixon are spelled out in the brochure about the center given to me upon arrival—to provide quality natural resource education, a base for forest product research, and manage the resources of the center wisely and economically. For the first three decades Rhett carried out these objectives at Solon Dixon, where the center provided opportunities for Auburn students and faculty to conduct research on forests and wildlife, and each year for classes to visit from the main campus and about ten other universities. Figuring out how to consistently make money at the center was more difficult. When Mr. Dixon gave the land to Auburn, many of the big trees had been removed years earlier and most of the acreage was occupied by low-quality natural stands of mixed pines and hardwoods.

As Solon Dixon's first director, Rhett continued traditional timber harvesting, managed an existing pecan grove and a cowherd, and leased some of the land for farming to add income, but over the years Rhett became more and more interested in the possibilities of native longleaf pine, a species that had been eradicated from 90 percent of its original range. He began experimenting with longleaf forestry, planting large stretches of Solon Dixon in the trees. "Mr. Dixon told me he could remember longleaf pine as far as he could see," Rhett explained as we walked around the center on the first day. "The land was clear-cut in the forties and fifties and never planted back until I got serious about it in 1981."

Out of Rhett's experimentation with longleaf came the Long Leaf Alliance, an organization based at Solon Dixon whose mission is to return longleaf to large areas of its former range. When Rhett retired from Solon Dixon he became the president of the alliance full time, and only recently had he cut back on his responsibilities there, giving him some time to show us around.

Rhett is short and compact with a silver, well-trimmed beard. His melodious lowcountry South Carolina drawl is smooth as a sip of expensive bourbon, and when he tells stories (which he does often) you're drawn into an oral tradition deep as a cypress swamp. Rather than talk like a professor (which he has been from time to time) Rhett told us stories about the early days at the center, how he and his family lived at the isolated forestry outpost "a beer and a half" from town, but actually had little reason to go into Andalusia except for groceries. "For a long time I had a five-thousand-acre backyard," Rhett said.

When it comes to southern conservation, Rhett's vision is wide ranging. As we got oriented to Solon Dixon, he listened and tolerated my desire for an ecological Eden not limited by practical concerns like keeping the lights on, but Rhett also knows how to talk to those who see land as a commodity, a numbers game. He reminded me a little of a southern version of Aldo Leopold, a man who started out teaching forestry and then took on the complex, on-the-ground long-term restoration of a local landscape.

The last of the center's objectives—wise management—is achieved through the property serving double duty as research facility and hunt club. The arrangement is a sort of legacy of the days before Solon Dixon was founded. Mr. Dixon was a member of a hunt club, and when he donated the property the university kept that relationship.

When Mr. Dixon died, Solon Dixon needed the income, so a club continued to operate on the property. The hunting lease is a small portion of the income stream, but because of the responsibility of providing a quality deer herd, coyotes have come under suspicion by the members on Solon Dixon as they have everywhere else in the South. The deer hunters saw their presence as troublesome as soon as research like John Kilgo's began to suggest that coyotes have a significant impact on deer fawns. "They shoot hogs on sight," Rhett explained. "Occasionally they kill a bobcat or a fox, but without fail they'll shoot a coyote if they see one."

There is nothing wrong with having management objectives, but I saw right away that this was no African wilderness, and, if troublesome to someone or something more desirable, the coyotes could easily be managed out of the equations and formulas. This was brought into focus when Rhett told a story about how three years earlier folks in the hunt club began reading the fawn mortality studies and extrapolating on the data gathered in South Carolina and elsewhere and developing their own fears about the Solon Dixon deer herd. "The hunt club members started asking me, 'What are y'all going to do about these coyotes?'" Rhett said. "Everybody was concerned about deer recruitment. That's when we decided to try trapping."

The night after Mike and I arrived we met with Rhett and Joel Martin, a Wofford College biology graduate who had followed Rhett as director of Solon Dixon. Like Rhett, Joel extended the center's hospitality, and when he expressed interest in my coyote project I tried to explain to him what I was up to. I said, "I'm not a scientist or a journalist. I'm just interested in what people have observed or heard about coyotes in Alabama and all over the South. I hope to try and write a first-person account that makes three things clear—they're here, they're not going away, and there are many ideas about how we should handle our relationship with them."

"They're here alright," Joel said, and then he offered up some opinions as we sat in one of the center's classroom buildings. When I asked him how Alabama hunters were reacting to the research on fawn predation by coyotes, if they were extrapolating based on the research in South Carolina, Joel laughed and said, "Deer hunters extrapolate on everything they hear. A few years ago *Deer Hunter* magazine published a picture of a black bear carrying off a fawn and all the hunters started screaming, 'We got to get rid of the black bears!'"

I asked him when he first heard about coyotes in Alabama. "We had coyotes when I got to Alabama eighteen years ago. It was obvious to me even back then that we'd have more," he said. "I used to hear a pack singing, but now when one bunch starts, they start up all over. I even see them in the daytime now. That's when I began to get serious on asking what I could learn about them. Now we have a whole bunch of them."

"Are you worried about them?"

"It's not the end of the world. I'm not that far into the Kool-Aid yet."

"Once they moved in, the population moved up steadily," Rhett added. "It's moved up and maybe it's peaked."

"Yeah, I started noticing about three years ago that when we had a hunter lose a deer you'd find it in the morning and there would be nothing left but the head," Joel said.

"In Texas they say, 'For every doe the coyotes eat, that's one more we don't have to shoot,'" Rhett said.

"Don't the hunters see how coyotes could help shape a healthy deer herd?" I asked.

"For hunters too many deer is not enough," Joel said, laughing. "That's as close as it comes."

"Our club's problem is that we've overeducated the deer and undereducated the hunters in the last twenty years," Joel said. "In 1976 you wouldn't shoot a doe and you'd shoot every buck, no matter size or age. Do you want a lot of deer or big deer?"

"Then they got to the point of much more aggressive killing of bucks and saving does," Rhett said.

"Animals are smart," Joel said. "We told people for years we needed to reduce the deer population, but nobody ever heard that what that meant is that we're going to have to reduce the number of deer."

"Back to coyotes, most hunters feel they've have had an impact on the deer," Rhett said. "As Mark Twain said, 'I wouldn't have seen it, if I hadn't a thought it.'"

"More coyotes," Joel said. "That's part of the deer equation. But the deer mangers don't really know where it's going to fall yet. Can we knock coyotes back? I'm not sure. Once we trapped them we started catching a bunch of coyotes in the same place, but it doesn't seem to have knocked them back at all."

As we continued talking, Joel seemed more concerned about pigs than coyotes. "I feel certain we'll never get rid of coyotes or, worse, this plague of pigs," he'd said with some resignation.

Later that night we had dinner at Rhett's house in Andalusia. Rhett had invited Mark Bailey, an endangered species biologist, over to meet us. Mike and I sat around Rhett's living room with Mark and Rhett telling wildlife stories. Mark told one story of checking a small pond for frogs, and on the way out he heard coyotes open up all around him. "I know I wasn't in any danger, but it spooked me a little."

Then Rhett countered with a story about setting up an orienteering course on Solon Dixon and getting the feeling that coyotes were following him. "I ran back to the truck," Rhett said, leaking out the punch line like the expert storyteller he is. "I even broke off a pine knot to protect myself."

Listening to them tell stories I thought about how there are two types of people in the South now, those who are still close to the land and those who aren't. The ones who are—hunters, farmers, foresters, wildlife biologists, field scientists of various ilk, environmentalists, and the recreationalists—mostly see the coming of the coyotes along a continuum varying from anger to a sort of studied curiosity verging even at times on fascination. They're all apprehensive because they know the coyote is a new animal on the landscape and it's early in the game, and so we don't know much. Scientists will be the first to tell you they wouldn't try to predict what the result of the presence of coyotes will be yet. So far there is a deficit in what we know, and the quality and quantity is limited about the region's coyotes. "Information about populations, social behavior, home range, and foraging ecology are of particular priority, as this information is vital for wildlife managers to understand," one survey of eastern coyote literature states emphatically. Scientists do know, though, that the game, whatever it is, is definitely in motion and it's changing year to year.

Some folks interested in coyotes have more empathy for them than others. Most natural historians know that the South has been swept over by species expansions before, whether it was the boll weevil, kudzu, armadillos, white-tailed deer, beavers, or *Homo sapiens*. Southerners have always been tagged as a people with a strong sense of place, and part of that is founded on figuring out how to deal with what environmental historian William Cronin calls "changes in the land." Solon Dixon is no different. It's a landscape that's been cut over at least several times with centuries of other human uses shaping its woods and fields.

Our second morning at the center, Rhett introduced us to Larry Stallings, and I knew I was finally onto something that could be at the heart of my Solon Dixon story. Once the decision was made to trap, Larry Stallings became Solon Dixon's point man. "Larry knows more about coyotes than anyone around," Rhett explained.

Larry is slender and works the property crew in a green brimmed hat and square-framed glasses. Maybe it's the hat, but when we met he looked like someone who could be a direct descendant of Hank Williams, whose childhood home is less than twenty miles away. Larry's lived in that county all his life and told me he'd caught his first coyote thirty years earlier, but "back then nobody knew what it was." Larry thinks the coyotes have been fully established in this part of Alabama for about fifteen years. "Some say they come in with the armadillos," he said.

Since we were on armadillos I asked Larry if the coyotes eat them: "Oh, a coyote will work an armadillo," Larry said. "There's hulls all over the fields up where I live. If they can catch 'em in a wide open field they can roll 'em over. I got two or three yard dogs and they'll run 'em but can't roll 'em. Coyotes have learned to flip 'em. I've seen a lot of bobtailed armadillos. I think the coyotes do that. You ever tried to pull a armadillo out of a hole?"

As we drove in Larry's truck I asked about how he came to trapping. "I had an uncle that taught me a little but I learned mostly by the seat of my pants."

Mike chimed in and said that he'd heard coyotes are hard to trap and Larry said, "It's time consuming. And there is no incentive now. Not enough people that's good enough to trap 'em. My best success is a trap that's been out for two weeks or better. I had my best luck when the weather has set in on them."

Mike wanted to know about bait, and Larry said, "We did good with fish slurry. That was a good call when we tried that."

"What's the strangest Alabama coyote story you've ever heard?" I asked, and Larry told me a story about a local fox pen:

"I wouldn't have believed this had I not seen it myself, but a feller caught a coyote on a snare on the Shoal River Range in Florida, about sixty-five miles by road from here. You can snare 'em down there. He snared this one in a culvert under the interstate. This coyote's left front foot and leg was white. He brought him up here and sold it for one hundred dollars to the fox pen, and after they put it in the holding tank and cropped its tail it got away, and one week later that same Florida feller catches the same coyote in the same trap. He brings the coyote back up and sells it to the same fox pen owner for a hundred dollars. The coyote gets away one more time and three weeks later the same guy catches the same coyote in the same snare. The third time the fox pen owner pays the a hundred dollars and says, 'You put that coyote in my dog box,' and when he does he walks over and shoots it. 'I can't keep paying over and over for that same damn coyote . . .'"

Larry slowed the truck and pointed down an overgrown road disappearing into the pines. "I usually place one set ten steps up in there so I can see it if I slow down. You check the traps early—people will spot 'em up in there."

I asked for more details and Larry said, "I caught fifteen males up in there before I caught a female. After that, it was one and one."

When Larry turned east off the main highway the truck bumped down a two-track through a field's center.

"What do you call this place?" I asked.

"We call it Danny's Field," Larry said. "Danny's the farmer who leases it."

Soon we reached a line of loblolly pines in the middle of Danny's Field and hard shadows fell in the two-track. Ahead of the truck the bright sandy field was hexed with a set of dark bars laid out along the tree line's long, steady length.

In 1912, just west of where we sat talking coyotes in a fallow Alabama field, there lived a woman named May Jordan. May was dirt poor and twenty-three years old, but she kept an extensive diary for two years of her father's trips from their home in Washington County through southwestern Alabama to buy furs. May describes her father's trade in the skins of plentiful muskrats, raccoons, opossums, minks, skunks, otters, and bears. She only mentions deerskins once in her diary, and catamounts and lynx were already very rare.

Coyotes were still fifty years in Alabama's future, but it's interesting to consider May's reflections on the raw rural lands and spotty wilderness of pine forests and swamps around her. It's the sort of landscape reassembled on the Solon Dixon property. "The sun rose bright and clear after the rain last night," she writes on February 7, 1914, in clear prose hard as pitch pine. "There is plenty of water ever place. And the frogs are singing in the swamps."

I read May's diaries with great affection and searched for a counterpoint to Larry's Solon Dixon coyote stories, but realized there isn't as much distance as I would assume between May's reflections on a hardscrabble land and Larry's stories of coyotes hunting armadillos in the fields near his house. May and Larry both know the local land and its animals from the inside. Like Larry, May understood the complex and practical relationship of poor rural southerners to wild animals. They are participants in a local natural economy. "All the poor animals are sure getting into trouble for Ever body is trapping and hunting," May writes on January 11, 1914. There is nothing romantic in her observations, though she does conjure a story on that same day in which she overhears a council of animals talking about how to avoid getting trapped and losing their pelts to her father.

Only three years earlier (1909) and two thousand miles west, Aldo Leopold had experienced the dying Mexican wolf that led to his most famous essay. May doesn't come close to describing anything that could be seen as a "fierce green fire" lingering in the cold dead eyes of the thousands of animal carcasses and hides she sees loaded onto her father's wagon.

I took in the sandy fallow field ahead of us stretching into the distance, and it looked like land May Jordan would recognize. This was an archetypical Deep South agricultural landscape—field, tree line of mixed hardwood and pine, and the rusty gabled tin top of a single farmhouse, this one in the next field and barely visible over the trees.

"We call this Rome, Rome plantation," Larry said, pointing past me to the housetop I'd spotted. "I've caught thirty-two coyotes here in a half-mile radius."

"Thirty-two?" I asked, writing the exact number in my notes. I was thinking that's a lot of coyotes, even for lower Alabama, a place where they have been present for decades.

"Thirty-two," Larry repeated.

I looked out at the tree line. The northern edge of Danny's Field must have been some coyote interstate highway. I wrote a note wondering if there was any way to know why this was Larry's sweet spot. Had Larry stumbled upon some canine trapping epicenter? Did every traveling coyote in that hard-edged farming country pass these pines on its daily rounds? It was hard to believe Larry caught the only thirty-two coyotes in the county, but I asked him again and he repeated the number.

In a couple of hundred yards Larry stopped the truck. "This is the best spot," he said. "I caught twelve right here."

I looked around. We were hard up against brush bordering the pines. Dewberry bloomed in the hedge. Dried climbing fern formed a brown scum on top of evergreen privet. There seemed to be nothing special about the place besides its rural handsomeness and the high coyote count. The tree line was one of half a dozen sharp edges between forest and field I could see from the cab of the truck. This coyote honey hole was serene and pastoral. Larry turned off the truck and we got out.

"You see there," Larry said, pointing to the sandy ground. "There was two through here earlier today. One morning I put out two traps here and it was the only time I've ever been 100 percent."

Mike quizzed Larry about his timing. You could tell Mike was weighing what he knows about trapping in the South Carolina piedmont to what Larry does in Alabama. Did he have luck on the first night? Mike asked.

"The second night is the best. If it rains and you can get out the next morning and check the set, it works."

I looked down and saw the distinctive slender nailed tracks of the two coyotes walking west toward the paved road.

"Just like deer," Mike said. "You find a certain spot and they'll cross it over and over."

"What tipped you off to here?" I asked.

"What made me find it was this real sandy spot and I saw they'd been playing in it."

"You ever had a deer step in a trap?" Mike asked.

"Yep, but all I got was hair."

Larry walked to the back of the truck and dropped the tailgate. A set of posthole diggers and two traps were laid out in the truck bed next to a five-gallon pickle bucket holding a hatchet, a beat-up wooden square screen for sifting soil, several lengths of rebar stakes with a washer welded to the top, a trowel, and a gob of old insulation. "I had one set below the house and I tried and tried to get him and then one day I left the hammer out there when I was setting traps." He pulled his hammer out of the bucket and showed the handle to me. "He chewed on that handle and that day I had him."

Mike picked up one of Larry's closed traps. It looked like the superstructure of a mechanical clam when closed. When I asked, Mike said, "This is a one-and-three-quarter-inch coil spring. Some people call it a double-coil spring." Mike bent the dark muddy jaws down with his bare hands and set the trigger. Larry worked on the other trap with a set of metal spreaders, opening the jaws wide and engaging the trigger.

Larry dug a hole in the sand and placed the trap. "If a fox or a coyote springs one of these and gets away I call him educated. Once they're educated they're hard to catch."

Larry and Mike got into a discussion about chain length as Larry measured off the distance he liked to set the trap from the stake.

"Everybody does it different. After you do it so many times and it doesn't work you find something that does and you stick with it," Larry explained.

Mike nodded his head, and said, "I understand your philosophy on it."

As Larry prepared his demo trap set we saw Rhett's F-150 silver crew cab coming through Danny's Field. After creeping to a halt and saying hello, Rhett fell into an easy conversation with Larry about the history of Danny's Field.

"When Hurricane Opal came through in '95 there were thirteen hundred and forty-seven eighty-year-old pecan trees here. Once the wind died down there were only twenty standing. Those pecans were like sails in that wind."

"Now they're growing cotton, corn, peanuts," Larry said, still working to set the trap. "Eighty-five acres."

"It was a mess and brought our pecan operation to a halt."

"Well, there it is," Larry said, looking down at the trap set he'd set in the sand. He picked up a stick and sprang the trap. The jaws snapped shut, and he said simply, "That's how I do it."

Over the next hour Rhett drove us in a circuitous route to a place he called the Iron Rock. We took secondary roads through the Alabama countryside. Going from place to place was a little like listening to Rhett's storytelling had been. Nothing ever went in a straight line, but in the end, you always arrived at something memorable.

In the Conecuh National Forest Rhett stopped to show us a research stand of longleaf for endangered red-cockaded woodpeckers where the trees had been marked with white slashes. We walked through the winter wire grass, gall berry, yaupon, and brown sedge, and looked up at woodpecker holes guarded by slicks of resin that helped keep the rat snakes from pilfering the nests in the spring.

"They drill into live trees," Rhett explained. "They need to have enough heart wood to make a cavity."

We saw three birds in five minutes flying over, a hopeful sign for the return of the longleaf ecosystem.

"They live in family groups," Rhett explained. "They're territorial and will defend against other woodpeckers."

"Like coyotes," I said.

Back on the Solon Dixon property we took the sandy two-track toward the river. Iron Rock stands out in the pine forest, a slight rise on the ridgetop of rusty stone before the incline to the river, like a jagged dirty fingernail pointed at the sky. A controlled burn had passed through recently and flame-tolerant longleaf stubbled the slope in front of the rock. "I often see snakes sunning here in the winter," Rhett said. "We ought to check it out."

We stepped out of the truck and circled the rock. Rhett and Mike went one way and I went the other. I like being in the woods alone. It reminds me why I got interested in this coyote story to begin with, to get out in the woods with new and old friends, to see the southern landscape close-up, and to learn what I could about its inhabitants. My pants were soon smudged with charcoal from the recent controlled burn, and when I looked down, each khaki leg was a Japanese Sumi painting framed with the burned saplings' delicate brushstrokes.

The thin soil had ash blowing about and the air still smelled burned, though Rhett explained as we drove up that the fire had passed through more than a week before. The blue sky and white ash swirled together as I walked slowly along the base of the hill and then circled up toward the summit. Prickly pear was the only thing green that survived the blaze.

As I approached the rocky summit I saw that the slabs of slanted rocks formed a small cave, and it was obvious as I walked closer that I had stumbled on the active den site of some animal. I looked in the soil around the entrance and saw the distinct tracks of a coyote like what I'd seen on the trail behind our house and what Larry had pointed out in Danny's Field earlier. On our last day we had stumbled upon a coyote den. I yelled for Rhett and Mike, and they met me at the opening. I leaned down, but the passage turned and I couldn't see inside.

"That's a nice den," Rhett said. "I don't think I'll tell Larry what we found. I might come back out here and put a camera on it."

"You know the fawn drop coincides with their pup drop," Rhett said. "Ironic that through the years we said we got to do something to kill off all these deer. They've survived night hunting, extended season, no bag limits. But you let coyotes kill off a few fawns and everybody hits the panic button."

Standing around the entrance to the den we talked a little more about coyotes. We wondered about their lives at Solon Dixon and how clear it was that they are here to stay. Mike kneeled and looked closely at the prints and scratches around the den's entrance and checked the hole's orientation to the sun—south facing. "I've always admired something that can come that far and adjust to anything we throw at them," Rhett said. "I don't condemn them. They've got their place, and they're here."

Suburban Coyote

Symptoms of Phobia of Coyotes: breathlessness, excessive
sweating, dry mouth, shaking, heart palpitations, inability
to speak or think clearly, a fear of dying, becoming mad or
losing control, a sensation of detachment from reality or a
full blown anxiety attack.—from a website

Walking with Meredith Doster around Atlanta's Druid Hills
on a steamy August afternoon I wasn't surprised that coyotes could
flourish there. The original map of Druid Hills shows a neighborhood
shaped like a river system, running east–west, what their official history calls "a linear version of the traditional village green," where the
parks intersecting the main corridor—Ponce De Leon Drive—range
from "relatively open greenswards to nearly impenetrable woods." The
neighborhood was originally laid out by Frederick Law Olmsted in the
late nineteenth century so that Atlantians could have "healthful living
in a country setting, yet not far from the city."

Meredith had moved to what she calls "the great Atlanta sprawl,"
from Arkansas. She and her husband chose to live within walking distance of Emory University and settled in Druid Hills. On her blog
she observed that "reverberations of Olmsted's designs are surfacing
today in Druid Hills," and noted how the "country setting" with wide
corridors of green space is perfect habit for "a band of coyotes whose
presence is testing the limits of Olmsted's bucolic vision."

How perfect. How could I pass up a chance to write about a
place named Druid Hills? What better landscape to outline the

contemporary coyote suburban–urban conflicts that will compli-
cate the politics of neighborhood associations at least until another
great comet strike puts all planetary issues into perspective? Maybe
Olmsted had druids in mind to roam these woods and vales, but it
also has proven perfect for creatures of the wooded margins—fox,
raccoon, opossum, mice, white-tailed deer, hawks, owls, and, more
recently, and to a greater degree than anyone would ever believe, pioneering coyotes.

This was eastern suburban forest at its best, the perfect habitat for
wild, weedy species like the coyote, good at living in close proximity to
us. On the main roads through the suburb there were stately homes on
huge lots thick with hundred-year-old poplars and oaks, deep brushy
swales with small rivulets tricking down to Lullwater Creek, and
narrow common-land alleyways connecting street to street, laid out
a century earlier for access by domestics, but now probably prowled
more often by foraging wildlife.

"We moved to this neighborhood because of the trees," Meredith
said as we paused in front of a lawn on Oakdale Road.

Though she and her husband had moved from the neighborhood
a year earlier, Meredith could still recall the spot they had first seen
a suburban Atlanta coyote. "We were in the car with our two dogs."
One of the dogs gave what she calls "that fox or coyote bark," and sure
enough, "there was a coyote running through this very yard."

By that time, Meredith's sensitivity had already been raised to coyote presences in the neighborhood, so she wasn't surprised or scared
since they had big dogs and with her Arkansas connections, she was
no stranger to coyotes. "It wasn't dusk though," she added. "And it
wasn't early morning either. I remember thinking it was an odd time
to see a coyote out in the open."

I didn't tell Meredith, but I've kept a Google Alert under the term
"coyote attack" for over three years. Gruesome stories from all over
the United States have filled my in-box every morning. I've read about
the maulings of suburban Chihuahuas named Slug, Little Bit, Jake,

LuLu, Teddy, and Chicita. There was a Yorkshire terrier named Fred, an eight-year-old pug named Molly, and a twelve-year-old cockapoo named Rudy. Rudy had survived but was so chewed up he needed a feeding tube inserted for meals. Another alert brought news of Mai Tai, a Siamese cat now missing his entire front leg.

Day by day, week by week, month by month, there were more: Sebastian and Sasha the Maltese, Chachi the little schnoodle, and Trixxie the black Chiweenie. There was the Maltipoo named Daisy, and the black teacup Pomeranian named Pippy.

Six-year-old Zoe, a Chihuahua, was gone in an instant from a suburban backyard—mauled and dragged into a ravine. "I saw a flash of brown, a flash of grey," her owner explained. "I saw it come over the fence and land and pounce right on the dog. Grabbed it by the scruff of the neck and tore up the hill."

And there was Cleopatra, the poodle, outside on her long leash when her owner heard the scream. "I pulled the leash and all that came back was her dog tags."

As I read each story I thought about these reported casualties of the suburban and urban coyote wars, and at first I was shocked. I have Murphy, my own overweight beagle, and I can't imagine the terror of seeing him attacked and dragged off. And I thought of all those old folks who have lost their animal companions, and the unsuspecting urban and suburban dwellers who thought their backyards were safe zones with no wildlife more dangerous than fire ants, only to see their pets disappear.

But sometimes my sentiments reverse for a perverse moment, and I imagine the engineered miniature canines with their absurd names from the coyote's point of view, these perfectly sized little protein packages tenderized by fourteen thousand years of human breeding and bled of what little fight they may naturally have possessed—coyote city cousins, underchallenged kinfolk offered up as easily hauled, meal-sized stand-ins for wild food, well-tended pets processed by domesticity, well done, and ready for the pickin'.

The coyotes don't always win. There are heroic stories of dogs defending other dogs against the coyote hordes ranging in from the wild. Out in California, Ronnie, a wire fox terrier, a normally shy dog, fought off a coyote to protect its backyard companion, a smaller silky terrier. The coyote jumped a six-foot wall to get into the backyard. "Ronnie was named for one of my heroes, Ronald Reagan," his owner told the local news channel. "Now Ronnie's my hero too."

But the loss of all these pets is just a symptom of a creeping national issue—the collision of the domestic and the returning wild taking place all over our urbanizing and suburbanizing country, and specifically for my purposes here, in the South. During the years of my travels coyote conflicts, usually prompted by the disappearance of pets—dogs and, even more often, cats—have ignited in many southern cities—including Birmingham, Charlotte, Charleston, and Atlanta.

Many communities are feeling the impact of the new omnivore on the block. On the south side of Charlotte a rare, rabid coyote sent a whole neighborhood into lockdown for a week, and in Carrboro, North Carolina, one resident wrote after a daylight encounter with a coyote, "It's super scary. I feel like we're being besieged and held hostage."

"If you believe our neighborhood listserv, then every house in Five Points has its own coyote," one friend wrote when I asked her about the issue in Athens, Georgia. On Sullivan's Island outside of Charleston another friend sent a local news story about how a group of residents had hired a trapper and one group is suing the city to remove forest cover from public lands. My friend wrote, "*Jaws* was on TV last night. The panic, the fear, and especially the concern over financial losses all rang a bell—rang the coyote bell. The argument used to be that the view-blocking maritime forest has reduced the value of a beach-front lot, and now it's the view-blocking, DANGEROUS maritime forest."

Down the coast in Hilton Head, the Sea Pines coyotes prompted the printing of T-shirts that say "Let 'Em Howl" on the front and "Save the Sea Pines Coyotes" on the back to support their presence, while another group of residents is cheering on an old-time island predator, the alligator, with a report of one cornering a coyote.

Battle lines have been drawn, but there's little agreement on how to fight, much less win, the suburban coyote war, or even if there is a war. One side says we have to learn to live with the coyotes. "For the folks who are very concerned about the coyotes and would like them trapped," one southern city manager explained to the press after an attack, "there is an equal number who believe the natural environment should be protected." The other side says secure the perimeter. Stay on the offensive. Hunt. Trap. Carry bear spray or foghorns when strolling through green spaces to ward the coyotes off and keep your pets safe.

The fear of rabies often inflames the anticoyote sentiment. A couple of years ago when the coyote scares were raging in Charlotte a coyote jumped a backyard fence bordering a greenway and attacked a large pet dog. Though they did not run tests, animal control assumed the animal was rabid. The owner of the pet said she now understands "nature can come right up" to her back door, and you never know "what's back there."

Yes, rabies is out—or "back"—there, one of those viruses we share the planet with, and wildlife is its most common host. Wildlife accounts for most of the rabies cases in United States, and any mammal can become infected—groundhogs, beavers, and even otters. Though the disease occurs in coyotes, rabies is much more common in raccoons, skunks, bats, and foxes. In North Carolina in 2013 there were over four thousand animals tested for rabies and none of them were coyotes. This isn't to suggest that the threat of rabies should be ignored, just that using the coyotes-carry-rabies-therefore-coyotes-should-be-eliminated-from-our-landscape argument falls logically short.

Rabies is, and will always be, one of the challenges we face with coyotes. In Texas the threat of rabies to coyotes has been mitigated by distribution of bait laced with vaccine. This is much cheaper and more humane than antiquated ideas about the elimination of the offending species.

But how can we settle the issue of suburban and urban coyotes? It's vast, like the suburbs and cities themselves. In my search for city coyotes I decided to focus on Atlanta, the region's largest metro area, and so I followed an early lead to Meredith.

We continued our walk on down Lullwater Road, the street *Driving Miss Daisy* was filmed on, and turned to enter the narrow greenspace called Lullwater Bird Preserve. "It's here they say some of the traps were set," Meredith said, pausing by the creek.

Only a few years earlier Druid Hills had become the epicenter of coyote skirmishes in the South to such an extent that the *New York Times* published an article noting, "The urban coyote problem has come to Atlanta at last." Druid Hills dealt with their "coyote problem" in a way unique to southern communities, and it speaks to the complexities of the issue and also to the diversity of opinions maybe only available in suburban Atlanta near a major university. After various reports of missing pets and coyote sightings, the neighborhood civic association sponsored a community meeting in early 2013. The forum included an impressive spread of experts and practitioners, Chip Eliot, a local professional trapper; Dr. Chris Mowry, a Berry College biologist; and Mary Paglieri, a human–animal conflict resolution expert from California. The topic of the meeting was listed as "coexistence," and it was cosponsored by a group called Coyote Coexistence Atlanta.

The suburban trapper had twenty years' experience, but he seemed a little nervous and talked of both educating the public and the removal of the animals. He started painting a verbal picture of an "in-town coyote," a male, moving through the neighborhood. "A coyote [pronounced 'ky-yote' like a westerner], when he heads out for the evening, his main goal is looking for food—when he's traveling through an urban area there's food everywhere, a buffet out there for him."

The trapper described the coyote's food choices—cat food, fruit, acorns, mice, rabbits, any rodent, garbage, roadkill, and feral cats, even watermelons. "They'll eat up some watermelons," he said, scoring laughter from the audience. And then he brought up pets—"Cats and dogs—they're doomed. They really don't stand a chance."

I guess I shouldn't have expected a character from *Duck Dynasty*, but the urban trapper was very nicely dressed in a sweater and slacks, more like a manager of a dry cleaning shop or a pest control company than the other trappers I'd met in my travels. But he knew his stuff, though I noted that his explanation of the issue was very mainstream, much the way rural southerners would reasonably approach coyotes in the South—offer lethal control as the only option. He was not worried about the welfare of coyotes, though he made it clear that he considers himself a humane trapper and showed one of his traps to prove his point. He said that he understands and employs his profession's "best management practices." He said he sees the issue as territorial, a dispute between competing animals, us and them. "They don't own the place," he said at one point.

In the urban trapper's remaining time he endorsed "removal" for the neighborhood coyote problem but admitted that trapping would not eliminate the conflict, that it would only "knock them back" and only act as a control that could be exercised by humans. He explained how he believes trapping dampens the bold forays of coyotes into suburbs like Druid Hills. "Trapping puts fear back in them, and this fear can last four years in a community."

The biologist approached the podium next. He was dressed casually and was comfortable with the crowd, as you would expect a professor to be. He explained his research on coyotes and how he's interested professionally in urban and suburban coyotes in the South. He loaded up a Powerpoint presentation highlighting the natural history of the coyote's migration east, and he made it clear, as any good educator would, that what he wanted was to take this opportunity to educate. He clicked through slides on the various Canid species—timber wolf, red wolf, coyote, domestic dog—and even displayed a slide on evolution, and another on the need for more research on southern coyotes. "We don't understand the coyote in Atlanta very well," he said.

After the appeal for knocking the coyotes back from the urban trapper, and for more study from the professor, the animal–human conflict resolver walked up to the microphone. She'd done this before. She was confident. She had her own Powerpoint about her organization's work in California, and she clicked the first slide, said that what's happening in Druid Hills is not unusual. "Animal–human conflicts are happening all over the globe," she explained, and showed slides of elephants and people, cougars and people, coyotes and people.

Slide by slide, she pushed the idea of coexistence and behavior modification as a way to resolve the community's issues without killing. She confirmed what the trapper said, that coyotes are "feeders of opportunity," but insisted that they only feed on cats and dogs when the natural prey base was diminished by some natural disaster, something like a prolonged drought. She said that the research shows killing coyotes actually makes the situation worse, and explained how the coyote will simply fill back in the vacant territories; she presented the concept of modifying the behavior of humans and animals through harassment, or, as Meredith put it in her encapsulation of the animal–human conflict resolver's presentation on her blog, "to take coyotes seriously as participants in a community defined by all living beings that inhabit it—plant, human, and animal-life alike."

After the presentations by the three experts there was a question-and-answer period moderated by a neighborhood officer who was nervous about the conversation and moved things along quickly. There were a few questions about trapping that verged on hostility when the trapper refused to define what he meant by "euthanize the animals by state law" after they were caught. "Gunshot is not euthanasia," said one resident. The trapper walked away from the microphone and did not respond.

Several interesting exchanges unfolded between the trapper and the biologist, between the anecdotal universe and the scientific. One community member suggested that we should "trap the coyotes and then pee on them and let them go. Wouldn't that tell them we got another hierarchy here and you're not one of them?"

The biologist laughed, then answered, "That sounds nice in theory but as a biologist I'd say an organism wants to survive, wants to feed ... I would—just guessing here—I would say that would not be effective." Everybody laughed.

Then the suburban trapper told a story about coyotes passing on knowledge of individual animals in the pack "who go missing" after he had trapped them. An audience member asked the biologist if there is any scientific evidence to "conform to these anecdotes."

"As for what he's saying," the biologist said cautiously, "coyotes passing on information—I don't know of any studies, but I'm not contradicting what he's saying. I don't doubt it, that they are picking up that others are missing. I'm not familiar with studies that the information is passed along—this sort of gets hard at what I am saying, animals evolve."

I found much appealing about all three approaches, as I'm sure many in the audience did. I liked the variety of the trapper's practical techniques heavily based on his animal observations in the field, and I liked hearing the biologist say out loud what I had heard all over the South—we really don't know a great deal about coyotes here yet. They haven't been here that long, and there just hasn't been that much research. It doesn't always pay to extrapolate data gathered in one place to the whole southern landscape. Will resident coyotes in Atlanta behave like resident urban coyotes in Chicago, Boston, or Montreal? Maybe, but we don't know that for sure yet, and we will never know until someone like the biologist gets radio collars on those Druid Hills coyotes and tracks them through the wooded draws laid out a century before by Olmsted without coyote highways in mind.

I'll have to admit, the idea of coexistence with coyotes offered up by the animal–human conflict expert from California is the most appealing idea to me intellectually. I like the idea of living in the landscape with the coyote, though it has come up rarely as I have tracked

Coyote Nation's advance through the South. Plenty of folks are willing to say, "They're here and they're not going away," but I've only come across a few who would agree with Coyote Coexistence Atlanta and the woman from California that we should learn to coexist with them.

The most articulate and literary advocate of this sort of "dialogue" with other species to modify their behavior is another Californian, Derrick Jenson, and his *A Language Older Than Words*, a series of essays exploring interspecies communication. In the preface to his book, Jenson tells the story of altering a coyote's behavior at his California home by asking it in a reasoning voice to stop killing his chickens.

"The coyote did stop," Jenson insists, "and neither did it nor other pack members return." Jenson says he was skeptical, but after many more interactions with his local coyotes he saw this incident as the genesis of his long exploration of interspecies conversations. "There is a language older and far deeper than words," Jenson says. "It is the language of bodies, of body on body, wind on snow, rain on trees, wave on stone. It is the language of dream, gesture, symbol, memory. We have forgotten this language. We do not even remember it exists."

In *A Language Older Than Words*, Jenson goes into some detail about his conversations with his chicken-killing coyotes. He says the conversation began through intuition and luck, where much of our most important learning begins. Jenson simply called out to a coyote he happened to see in the brush at the edge of his yard, "Please don't eat the chickens. If you don't I will give you the head, feet, guts, whenever I kill one," he yelled. "And please don't forget my work in defense of the wild."

Jenson says the coyote simply turned and trotted away, looking back over its shoulder several times. "Except at night, to sing, the coyotes didn't come back for many months," he says, "and when at last they did, it was, it seemed, only to remind me to keep my end of the bargain."

What is to be learned about urban coyotes from Jenson's insistence that we have a conversation with the wild? This story goes against so much we've been taught to trust—especially for southerners. People generally believe there is a deep rift between us and the wild world, and that we are not to bridge it, and that if there is conflict, it needs not be solved with gunfire. The story of the Druid Hills coyotes brings so much of the issue into high relief.

Neighbors at the community meeting claimed dogs had been caught in traps, and as I walked with Meredith through Druid Hills I could see there were plenty of dogs walking in the park. I could also see why the neighborhood was worried about the trapping. We passed three or four couples walking dogs on the wooded trail, and Meredith said she and her friends often walked their dogs there and even let them run off-leash, even though they weren't supposed to.

It is natural for coyotes to take advantage of a small green space like the Lullwater Bird Preserve. They could den in an out-of-the-way log, or under a rock in an outcrop, and forage unseen among the houses at night, or even, if, as Meredith and her husband had seen, more advantageous, in the middle of the day. As the trapper had said, in an urban area there's food everywhere, and it's "a buffet out there."

"Did you ever hear them calling?" I asked Meredith.

"A couple of times."

"How did your neighbors react?"

"This neighborhood prides itself on being part of the landscape, but when the landscape bites back it gets tricky," Meredith said as she waded into Lullwater Creek to cool her feet on a hot summer day. She looked up into the wooded acres of the narrow creek valley and smiled. I guess you could say, I thought as I watched Meredith wading in the creek, the hills are alive with the sound of coyotes.

Miscegenation

Life finds a way.—Jeff Goldblum, *Jurassic Park* (1993)

Just before dawn in early April I headed out into the Alligator River National Wildlife Refuge in far eastern North Carolina. The vehicle thermometer showed forty degrees outside, and relentless winter-like conditions had already broken the hearts of many a young vacation reveler on Nags Head, where I was staying with my wife, Betsy. I worried the dipping Siberian air would have a negative impact on my early morning field trip. Do pioneering eastern coyotes and reintroduced red wolves hunker down on cold mornings? Soon after I'd crossed the bridge from Roanoke Island and the Outer Banks beyond, I spotted an overweight roaming yellow Labrador and, just down the road from the waddling dog, two deer browsing the roadside, so it looked like the ancient prey–predator dance I was searching for continued despite the unseasonal weather.

Riding the reserve roads was all I knew to do after driving four hundred miles from home to search for the coyotes and their red wolf cousins in the pocosin swamps—isolated coastal wetlands—of Dare County. It was late in the week and I was a little desperate. I'd come north to interview my friend Jan DeBlieu. I'd known Jan for twenty years. She lives on Roanoke Island and is the author of a number of natural history books, including *Meant to be Wild*, published in 1991, which contains one of the best long pieces on red wolves. The book is a study of reintroduced endangered species across North

America. She'd thought deeply about the hazards of reintroduction and hybridization.

I would see Jan later, but most of the reserve rangers and wolf researchers were either out of town or too overworked to answer e-mails or phone calls, and the only red wolves I'd seen were a stuffed adult and two pups in the new National Wildlife Refuge Visitor Center on Roanoke Island. I needed stronger narrative footing, for what could be the best (or worst, depending on your point of view) story about coyotes coming into the South out there. With this in mind, I got up at 4:30 a.m., layered up, and drove into the wild.

The Alligator River refuge was a perfect backdrop for a genetic drama: small enough for an exploration by road, large enough to contain the reestablishment dreams of government agencies. The refuge covers most of a fat coastal peninsula bordered on the west by the Alligator River and on the east by Croatan Sound. In a network of over a hundred wildlife reserves in the southern United States, Alligator River is the only place an eager hobby poet/mammologist like me might see three of the four North American canid species—*Canis lupus familiaris* (the Labrador), *Canis latrans* (the coyote), and *Canis rufus* (the red wolf). I looked forward to punching my life list with the red wolf, and tried to put off for a while the thorny scientific issue of species and hybridization. I knew from my preparatory reading there were those out there in science land who call this whole tribe of North American dogs (timber wolf, red wolf, coyote, domestic dog) a single species. Should I just leave it at that?

As I headed across two major bridges and motored west before dawn, I tried to think as deeply as I possibly could fueled by a single 7–Eleven honey bun and a cup of coffee about that distant county of the Carolinas and its relationship to the relentless push of coyotes into every corner of the region. Why Alligator River? Despite miles of Goofy Golf, outlet malls, and homogenized island sprawl only a good dose of climate change or one major hurricane away from Pick-up

Sticks and abandonment, I anticipated a rugged primordial fastness to that corner of eastern North Carolina. To add to the sense of isolation the U.S. Fish and Wildlife Services selected Alligator River for its bold wolf reintroduction program in the 1980s.

I half-listened as I drove to early morning NPR and sorted through facts, speculations, and uncertainties swirling through my vacating head. I laid out the coyote–red wolf issues at Alligator River. Since 1994 "genetic swamping" of the red wolf by the influx of coyotes has been labeled by the red wolf recovery team as one of the primary threats to the program. I wondered if I had the patience to attack the whole idea of species purity head-on, as in the past decade coyotes moving east and south have caught up with the isolated, reintroduced population of red wolves and their corner of the coast, and coyotes and wolves have begun again to interbreed, just as they had in the thickets and swamps of Louisiana and Texas before the last of the red wolves were extracted in the 1960s. In order to slow down the fraternization between wolves and coyotes, the U.S. Fish and Wildlife Service established a zone around Alligator River in which coyotes are trapped, sterilized, and then rereleased to take up with the wolves again. I'd thought of this zone as a DMZ, a place where the sterilized coyotes fill positions in the packs and run with the wolves and become "place holders" until the wolf packs increase in number and the pressure to breed with coyotes is diminished across the whole range. Would one of the best-known wildlife reintroduction projects on the planet survive this love affair between coyotes and wolves?

What is a species anyway? Biologists don't really know for sure, after centuries of defining and arguing on both philosophical and practical grounds. Shouldn't it be simple? Shouldn't it suffice to say a species is a distinct kind? Not so much. One approach to coming up with a definition, and probably the most common, at least in the past century, is that of reproductive barriers—populations of organisms similar enough to one another that they can potentially interbreed and produce viable young constitute a species. Populations of organisms that are further apart and cannot reproduce successfully do not. This criterion does not serve us when looking into species viability among canids though, as successful reproduction among dogs, wolves, and coyotes is possible, and even common, if the romantic atmosphere is right.

Another approach is to think of organisms changing through time and space. The whole pageant of life is, according to Stephen Jay Gould, like a bush pushing branches outward, filling up available space, with new species developing from a central trunk over time: "If each evolutionary line were like a long salami, then species would not be real and definable in time and space."

Though the definition of what constitutes a species has never been entirely settled, today most biologists are more interested in understanding the processes that go into speciation. "Speciation is usually a gradual process, so it is not unusual to encounter populations that are only partly reproductively isolated," explain the authors of the *Encyclopedia of Life*.

So, with my trip to Alligator River to learn about coyotes and wolves, Gould might say I was looking into the bush at just the right moment; I had pulled back the covers on an amorous band of mammals, cavorting together, forming bands, breeding, settling down, and raising offspring. The scientific chaperones weren't happy about it, but the canids were carrying on in spite of definitions.

The week before we'd arrived at Alligator River, Betsy and I had watched a PBS documentary called *Meet the Coywolf*, about the research surrounding the large hybrid carnivore moving steadily east and south. The program outlines how researchers have shown that this coyote-wolf hybridization is recent—developing in the last one hundred years or so—"an evolutionary blip in time" as they put it. Genetic work documents how the fraternization between species began in the wilderness of Algonquin Park in Ontario, Canada—but now the trail stretches east to Boston and New York, and south as far as Virginia.

"Something mysterious is moving through North America," the narrator intones. "Smart, adaptable, and watching our every move— meet the coywolf."

Though I knew it was a mistake to confabulate the timber wolf, the red wolf, and the coyote into a single story, the temptation was appealing, especially if I started to speculate about what the healthy population of wild canids might look like if genetic swapping and mate swapping continued over another one hundred years.

Human-altered habitat (clear-cuts, farmland, cities, suburbs) and climate change seemed to be increasing the likelihood that animals once thought distinct species might actually breed and create viable hybrids. If coyotes and wolves wanted to mate and add their genes to what the geneticists are now calling a "canid soup," could (or should) the federal government stop them? What flavor was in store for the soup? A hearty, chunky wolfish broth or a watery doggy gruel?

The morning's wild sugar-buzz was grounded a little at the intersection of U.S. 64 and state road 264, where a car was stopped in the middle of the road with hazard lights blinking. I slowed, rolled to a stop, and lowered my window. A man eased out from behind the wheel, ghostly in the pulse of the blinking yellow lights. He was Middle Eastern with a short-cropped beard and hair. I saw the panic in his eyes as he approached. He pointed at "bridge out" and "detour" signs and said something in broken English. He leaned into the open window and spoke more slowly when he saw I didn't understand, "What to do?" he asked.

Soon, his wife stepped out of the car and joined the man at the window in the dark and cold. She wore a gray scarf. "Greenville?" she said. "We go home to Greenville this way please?"

"We are here with no idea where to go," the man said a little more calmly, but with fear still in his voice. They both looked at me for deliverance. The black dawn yawned. A detour had turned a U.S. federal highway into the Dark Continent or a rewrite of *Strangers in a Strange Land*.

I explained the repairs ahead on the bridge. "Go this way," I said. "It will take over an hour longer, but you will get to Greenville if you travel on 264." They seemed relieved, and after I pulled off, in my rearview I saw the car's blinkers disappear and turn south.

Soon after sending these pilgrims on their way I'd stopped in my own pre-dawn darkness at the reserve kiosk on U.S. 64 for an over-sized trifold brochure, and I had it open on the seat beside me. I was as lost as the pilgrims in my fear and ignorance. What could I know for sure about this huge issue of genetic swamping, endangered species biology, conservation of wildlife, and federal law? I was a mere poet, albeit a curious one with a love for science and wildlife. I began by assessing the territory, my surroundings. I could see from the map that the peninsula was shaped like four fingers held up with a thumb folded back. Two-lane U.S. 64 pierced the reserve like an arrow flying from the east. A quarter of the reserve is above the highway and three quarters is below. North of 64 around South Lake there were few roads, but below the highway a dense grid of gravel roads opened access for my pre-dawn foray into red wolf country. That is where I would start my search for evidence of fraternization between coyotes and red wolves.

What should I do with these consorting ideas? Stay clear of them? Meet them head on? Throw them off the nearest bridge? Hide them away in the glove box?

I soon turned onto Milltail Road and passed the Creef Roadcut Trail and drove on down to Long Curve Road in the dark. As I crept along at fifteen miles per hour I could see cell towers blinking in every direction. My map showed me that in the center of the preserve the distance between roads is sometimes about two miles, with a half mile being more the rule.

The roads are named for local plants and animals—Bay, Blueberry, Cypress, Bear (and a shorter one nearby named Cub), Bobcat, Possum. The core of the preserve is a vast expanse of agricultural fields used for both production of vegetables and flooded fields planted with food crops for migrating waterfowl.

I had the windows rolled down and it was cold. I drove slowly and strained to see into the dark, with hopes I'd see a shadowy figure moving along the tree line. I glanced down at the seat beside me where I had opened my journal to a list I'd made earlier of the unanswered questions I had about the red wolf story: How does the DMZ between the advancing coyotes and the hunkered-down wolves really work? How successful have the biologists been in keeping more coyote genes out of the soup? If they can breed, what's to stop them from getting to it? How much mixing of genes is enough so that you have to call an animal a hybrid? Have the wolves shown interest in watermelons as coyotes do? Have Alligator River wolves shown the same taste for fawns that eastern coyotes have?

It was not as if this drive in the predawn chill was going to answer any of these questions, but they were intriguing to ponder. Dividing coyotes from wolves sounds like it would be an easy distinction, but I've discovered otherwise. The division is weighted with political importance, for there is another very interesting story intertwined with the coyote range extension I've been following through the South, that of the status, genetic pedigree, and reintroduction of the red wolf.

As I drove the preserve I went over in my mind what I had learned of the complex red wolf story. I had an inch-thick folder of peer-reviewed articles, popular magazine pieces and book chapters, and I had finished T. Delene Beeland's recent *The Secret World of Red Wolves*, an extensively researched and thoughtful assessment of the situation facing both the red wolves and the red wolf reintroduction project. Reading the multiple articles published about the project and the wolves had convinced me that what the world needs is not another official story about the fight to save what Beeland has called "North

America's other wolf," but it's still helpful to know the basic outlines of the story. In 1967 the red wolf was one of seventy-two species included on the original Endangered Species Act list. In 1968 the U.S. Fish and Wildlife Service showed or discovered that hybridization with coyotes had brought the last colony of red wolves on the coast of Louisiana and Texas close to extinction as a species, so from 1973 until 1980 the four hundred remaining red wolves were captured and culled for the "pure wolves" (using morphological standards or "if it looks like a wolf it must be a wolf," and later success and failure in breeding experiments), and the fourteen wolves they kept became the breeding stock for reintroduction into the wilds of coastal North Carolina. Then in 1980 U.S. Fish and Wildlife declared the red wolf extinct in the wild. The red wolves became the first animal documented to have become endangered by interbreeding with a separate species and also the first to be extirpated in the wild in order to save it from extinction and begin a captive breeding program.

Early releases were attempted on Bull Island in South Carolina, but the first full-scale release at Alligator River was on an early September morning in 1986. Biologist Michael Phillips wrote in his field journal, "We did it, we let them go," and the first experimental population of red wolves was established in northeastern North Carolina. This population was reintroduced on federal land, and they were monitored by way of radio collars, vaccinated against diseases, and evaluated after a trial period. By 1994 they had released sixty-three wolves in Alligator River.

In 1991 a second population of red wolves was established in Great Smoky Mountains National Park in eastern Tennessee. Chris Camuto wrote of this reintroduction in his *Another Country Journeying toward the Cherokee Mountains*. "The spaces between the mountains, empty for a hundred years, are now occupied by the howling of wolves . . . a subjective sound for the mountains to ponder, ridge to ridge," he wrote early on in that book. In 1998 the population in Tennessee was delisted because the wolves failed to establish home ranges in the park, where they couldn't find enough to eat. The promise that Christopher Camuto and others wrote about for wolves returning to the Cherokee Mountains disappeared as quickly as it materialized in the mountain fog.

One of the key figures in the biology and conservation, defining the red wolf as a separate species fighting for its recovery and reintroduction, was (now retired) U.S. Fish and Wildlife biologist Ron Nowak. Through publications and research Nowak almost single-handedly defined the red wolf as a separate species from the 1960s onward. Nowak looked at the long history of red wolf descriptions of naturalists in literature, including citations by William Bartram, John Bachman, and John James Audubon. He studied fossil skulls and compared them to historic contemporary skulls—five thousand in all. After his analysis Nowak believed that the red wolf had been a separate southern species for more than seven hundred thousand years.

Nowak and others pointed out that red wolves are smaller than gray wolves and bigger than coyotes; they have a more wolflike profile, with long, lanky legs and heavier bodies, big feet, bigger skulls, and longer snouts. More like a gray wolf than a coyote, their diet is more specialized too—mostly meat eaters, they stalk small mammals like rabbits, rodents, and raccoons, and even hunt deer.

But in the early 1990s geneticists such as Robert K. Wayne began using DNA analysis to define species as well. Through a number of influential papers they showed that a species was not so easy to define when you look closely at its genetic history, and that instead of being a separate species, red wolves have been a coyote/wolf hybrid for at least hundreds and possibly thousands of years. They suggested that conclusions by Nowak and others may not be supported by lab analysis, and that the expensive and controversial U.S. Fish and Wildlife program to maintain the "purity" of this single species may not make practical sense.

Nowak fought back by writing a number of long defenses of the red wolf as a distinct species. In 1995 he wrote: "The wolves of North

America are under a severe new threat from an influential group; not the lumber companies, fur trappers, or stockmen, but the zoologists, or at least some of them who are keen to publish claims that wolf populations have been hybridized with other species." Nowak felt that the geneticists were playing right into the hands of "commercial interests" who would seize upon this information to bring an end to conservation efforts so that an unpopular species could be exploited.

Nowak's position, that of an old-time naturalist/researcher who trusts judgments more complex than the display on a DNA sequencer, has lost power over the intervening two decades. Nowak retired from the service in 1997, shortly after the controversy over DNA and hybridization began.

Nowak has retired, but Robert Wayne and his colleagues continue their work. In 2011 Wayne published a paper in one of the leading genetic research journals on the sequencing of wolflike canids worldwide. The article is long and complex, but accompanying it is an attractive graphic, a colorful genome half-round, an open fan, with drawings of the canids in question at the top—a sweep of coyote green on the left, from "pure" western coyotes giving away to a tint of red wolf genes as you move toward the hybridization line where coyote/wolf becomes the red wolf; the red wolf's tiny slice of the wheel shows abundant green; the red wolf is followed as we go around the arc by "pure" blue timber wolves smack in the center (with the Rocky Mountain timber wolf being the purest), then onward across the Atlantic to yellow Eurasian wolves as we start down the slope on the other side, the red dogs (the squares speckled at margins with both wolf and coyote genes), but finally filling the whole far right with all their various breeds.

It's possible to stare at this image, as I did, and say, "Oh look, red wolves are genetically coyotes" due to the high percentage of coyote genes it looks like they carry in their slice of the genome. When translated into percentages Wayne and his colleagues put coyote versus wolf genes in the red wolf at about 76 percent (coyote) 24 percent (wolf).

What the image seems to show is that for thousands of years wolves and coyotes have traded genes—as have dogs and wolves and dogs and coyotes. Hence the "soup" among the canids that many researchers now talk about. Once when I laid out the complexities of the "canid soup" to one genetic biologist she said, "Oh, this hybridization that's happening to the coyotes, wolves, and dogs happens with most species over time. We're just lucky enough to see it in process with these canids."

Is this paper the last word on the genetic makeup of the red wolf? Not likely. As Delene Beeland says in her book on the red wolves, these disagreements over the animals origins are "acrimonious, divisive, deeply entrenched." She concludes that the truth (whether hybridization is the red wolf's beginning or its end) will likely remain elusive. Beeland's final word is that "we know without a doubt that when Europeans arrived in the New World, the eastern woods held howling chorusing wolves. But the not so simple question remains: what were they?"

As I drove around Alligator River, on the windswept eastern edge of the continent, the Red Wolf Recovery Program was still funded and the researchers were still fighting valiantly to preserve the so-called purity of the species, but in the intervening years since Nowak's retirement, coyotes had pushed defiantly into the territory of the precarious coastal North Carolina red wolves, bringing about the same situation that earlier researchers remedied by removing hybrids and reducing the "wolf" population to only fourteen breeding individuals.

Could researcher Michael Phillips have imagined that a mere twenty-five years after he uttered those hopeful and yet slightly sad words ("We did it, we let them go") that the red wolves would once again be muzzle to muzzle, or in the worst-case scenario, butt to butt, with their old Deep South and Wild West rivals, *Canis latrans*? As a good scientist, Phillips probably would have seen that one coming, but maybe not. As Jan DeBlieu added earlier on the phone when we were talking about the whole situation, "Who would have ever thought we'd be in this fix?"

The official position on southeastern coyotes by U.S. Fish and Wildlife ("the paradigm" as one scientific paper refers to it) was articulated this way in 2000 in an official technical report: "Extensive literature documents the havoc created by introducing species outside their historic range. . . . When species have not evolved together, effects such as excessive predation, excessive competition, unfamiliar disease and parasite transmission, etc. can be expected and can lead to extirpation of native species. . . . A good example is the coyote, which was originally found throughout most of the western half of North America. In conjunction with the extirpation of native wolves and land clearing in Eastern United States, the coyote has now extended its range eastward to the Atlantic Coast. However, personal experience and contacts with state wildlife agencies lead us to believe that introductions of coyotes by private citizens, most commonly to provide an animal to run with dogs, contributed more than natural expansion to this increase in range."

My morning did not yield any red wolf or coyote sightings. Dawn came and the roads and fields were empty and cold as the parking lots of the waterslides on Nags Head. The cell towers blinked red in the distance, the only sign of life in that desolate corner of federal land. I had seen nothing once the sun was up but two ghostly egrets taking off from a drainage ditch, a few mourning doves, and a pair of broad-winged hawks. I had heard only the whistle of killdeer and the "teep teep teep" of a woodcock. No wolves, no coyotes, though my heart had once raced when I made out on the gravel before me the muddy tracks of something large lumbering across the road not long before I had arrived.

When I returned from Alligator River later in the morning I called to invite Jan DeBlieu to come over to the beach house for a beer. When she arrived we talked about red wolves and coyotes for about an hour.

I told her about the muddy tracks on the road and she said it was probably a bear, a species that is doing very well in Alligator River. For the
many years I'd known Jan she had shown herself clearly as a defender
of all wild places and things. Like Derrick Jenson, she is a writer who
could yell at the wolves or coyotes, "And please don't forget my work
in defense of the wild!" In the long first section of *Meant to be Wild*
she creates an in-the-field narrative of red wolves as a native species
saved from extinction through captive breeding and restored to their
rightful place in her own backyard, this small corner of their original
natural range. Jan beautifully describes the rerelease of these wolves
and how in the late 1980s they had been granted "a provisional exis-
tence" by the extraordinary efforts of biologists. Their wildness and the
wildness in which they were released created a promise to be thankful
for. At the end of the section Jan stands before two stuffed red wolves
in a display at the Roanoke airport, two animals she had known as
living creatures before they died to be stuffed and displayed, and she
whispered "thank you" to the wolves for their sacrifice.

Now, decades later, Jan isn't quite so hopeful. Since she'd written
about the wolves they had almost entirely migrated out of the Alligator
River Preserve: "They just wouldn't stay," she explained. "The refuge
was carved out of the wettest, most inhospitable land in the region,
and as soon as they could the wolves voted with their feet, light-
ing out for the surrounding farmlands, which were dryer." This has
created its own set of social problems—a whole universe of public-
relations issues with local farmers as the wolves showed up (and set
up residence) on their land and the biologists relocated them and they
returned. And then there'd also been the whole coyote–wolf hybridization catastrophe of the last decade.

I'd asked Jan earlier if she was ambivalent about coyotes coming
into Alligator River. I was interested in her point of view, particularly
since she had written about the wolves twenty-five years earlier. Her
response seemed guarded: "For me, the coyote's infiltration in the East
is somewhat sad, because the species is filtering into the niche once

filled by wolves," she wrote back. "What we've got is a watered down version of a top predator, one that lives easily alongside people. They're beautiful, intelligent animals with a kind of mystique, and I'm happy to have some form of predator here. But still . . ."

When we sat down to talk I asked her again about her ambivalence, and she shook her head and wasn't quite so guarded. She took a sip of beer and compared coyotes to cockroaches. "I'm not ambivalent," she said seriously. "It's a tragedy."

"If you were writing your book today, how would you write the red wolf story?"

"I wouldn't be writing it today. This is no longer good red wolf habitat," she said.

I asked Jan what she meant. She took another sip of beer and explained the migration of the wolves out of the swamps and into the farmlands I'd read about, and she said it saddened her to watch a generalist like the coyote endanger the survival of a more specialized species like the red wolf. "This area was chosen because it was perfect to test out the reintroduction. This corner of North Carolina is one of the few places in the South biologists thought was wild enough to support a population of red wolves. One of the reasons they thought it would work here is that Alligator River is so wild no one had settled most of it. The land is so far from I-95 and there's so much water. The region not only has a vestige of its original wildness but it has ecosystems that can support the wolves. This area has always been different—peat and pocosin—not like anywhere on earth—a unique ecosystem hanging out here in the ocean. It's shaky ground, always has been. You have hearty people here who love being outside—ticks, chiggers, biting flies—that's why I loved the idea of wolves being here. If the wolves are driven to extinction because of hybridization with coyotes, it's the death of a dream."

Jan continued: "Can you have red wolves and coyotes living side by side? You'll have to ask the biologists that. I don't know. Even if the red wolf isn't genetically pure at this point, the animals we have now are the closest thing to the original wolf. In that sense they're worth holding onto. I understand the cunning Wile E. Coyote that can outsmart us—how cool is that? But what price would we pay if we lose the red wolf? If we lose the wolf here—then we lose the uniqueness of this place and wolves. If we lose the wolves we'll have lost the hard-won diversity we have again."

Before she left, Jan gave me contact information for a biologist in the red wolf program, and I got a chance to talk with her briefly the next day. I asked her about what I called the coyote–wolf DMZ, and she laughed at my metaphor, but I could hear in her voice that she was being very cautious with this poet who came out of left field with his metaphors. She said, yes, the zones are successful in the management, that there are fifty sterile coyotes in the red wolf recovery area, and that there are nine mixed packs. I fumbled for another question, and she explained I could look carefully at Fish and Wildlife's adaptive management plan if I wanted to understand the strategy more fully. "It's on the website and it's been updated quite regularly," she said. I told her I hadn't seen anything—bears, coyotes, wolves—on my morning drives, and she said, "Well, the wolves are starting to den."

When we ended our brief conversation I felt disappointed. Maybe I'd hoped the interview would have developed a little like the one filmmaker Werner Herzog had with the marine ecologist in Antarctica in which out of left field, Herzog asks about homosexual penguins:

Herzog: "I've read somewhere there are gay penguins. What are your observations?"

Researcher: "Um ... well ..."

Herzog's crazy question gave a slightly postmodern, decentering-science-from-itself spin to the entire encounter. My encounter with the on-site red wolf biologist made me accept what I already knew, that I would not be one of the dozens of journalists invited out to see the hidden wolf-release pens and to hear the full official story of the reintroduction from the agency's public relations staff.

I wasn't fooling myself, so why would I imagine I would fool any-one else? I'm not a journalist. If someone wanted to understand the red wolf reintroduction program they could read Beeland's *The Secret World of Red Wolves*, a balanced journalist's report, but that's not what I am getting at here. I'm a poet writing a book about coyotes coming into the South and how various people feel about it. I feared the researcher picked up right away that my interest is mostly in the randy, common coyotes, not the endangered red wolves. But coyotes are where it all started for me. Those wild howls in the backyard. Those thorny questions about what we would do backyard by backyard in the face of this occupation/colonization/range extension/dispersion/proliferation/invasion or, as I preferred, settlement. The biologists are probably mostly interested in the coyotes as a foil to something they want very badly, the successful reestablishment of an endangered spe-cies into its former range. But what I'm tracking is stories and feelings about a highly successful canine sweeping into an empty niche, and watching, as Deanna, the biologist in Barbara Kingsolver's *Prodigal Summer*, says, "a significant predator . . . sliding quietly into the niche vacated two hundred years ago by the red wolf."

But, all that said, I also had to remind myself, on a tiny fingernail of the continent the "niche" is not empty if the species defenders are right; it is filled by between 90 and 110 "red wolves" with the possibility of horny male coyotes sniffing after every wolf bitch that goes into heat. The program goes forward with clear objectives. The current recovery plan has been the same since 1990 and specifies very specific objec-tives, including to establish and maintain at least three restored red wolf projects within the species' historic range, to have the populations be large enough to have the potential for natural evolutionary pro-cesses to work within the species, among others.

Will the Alligator River experiment succeed? Will the biologists find a way to include the coyotes in their plans since they are not going away? I went back and read what Jan had say at the end of *Meant to be Wild*: "I continue to remember what I have learned from the wolves of Alligator River—that there is no way to predict how any wildlife restoration project will unfold, or how it may succeed. To be a conservationist is to be an eternal optimist."

Our last morning on Nags Head I was feeling optimistic, and so I drove with Betsy back out to Alligator River and we walked an asphalt trail and another gravel trail at Milltail Creek. The first trail was paved for handicapped access and arrow straight, made for the ecotourist trade. We didn't see much—mostly scat on the asphalt was what interested me. I took pictures of six or seven different deposits with my iPhone, using my blue pen for scale. Fascinating stuff. At least for me. It could have all been bear, or I hoped, maybe bear and wolf. One pile was full of fish scales, another small bird feathers. Betsy wasn't as interested in the scat as I was. She wanted to walk at a steady pace and get some exercise. She joked about my obsession with shit and took a picture of me squatting over one pile with my notebook, and we posted it on Facebook, bleeding a little more wildness from the encounter on the paved trail.

Hybridization sounds so scientific, I thought as we walked, like something that happens in a test tube. I played around with using a different cultural term: miscegenation, and the minute I formed the word in my mind it gave the whole mess a southern slant I'd always wanted to keep at the center of this story about coyotes.

Red wolves prefer their own, as the biologists put it, and only mate with coyotes when their "social affinities" break down, as happened in Louisiana and Texas in the 1960s and could happen again in North Carolina, if the hybridization cannot be controlled.

As we walked I recalled Faulkner's Uncle Buck and Uncle Buddy and the tumble and lurch of the short story "Was" in *Go Down, Moses*. It's 1859 in rural Mississippi, and in Faulkner's story the impossibly complex social drama of slaves, owners, and desire plays itself out against a backdrop of an escaped fox and an escaped slave.

"What in damn's hell do you mean turning that damn fox out with the dogs all loose in the house?" Uncle Buddy asks Uncle Buck.

"Damn the fox," Uncle Buck replies, and the fox and the dogs and "five or six sticks of firewood" come out of the kitchen and the fox trees behind the clock on the mantel. "Tomey's Turl has broke out again," and a repeated, darker hunt begins in the first few pages of Faulkner's cycle of stories of chasing the escaped slave Tomey's Turl from one farm to the next.

There are no coyotes or wolves in Faulkner that I remember, unless he fails to mention some brought back from out west for running the hounds. Instead, it's foxes that play the part of sometimes-comic persecuted quarry in his novels, and there are those images of the years just before he died up in Charlottesville as master of his own tally-ho hunt.

Later in the sequence of interrelated stories making up *Go Down, Moses* we discover there is a deep kinship complication with the men chasing Tomey's Turl down. Tomey's Turl is Buck and Buddy's half-brother, the son of their father, Lucius Quintus Carothers McCaslin, and his slave Tomey. I imagine the hunting dogs bred and traded all over the South, and I consider Faulkner's obsession with the ledger books outlining who begat who on the plantation—what we call kinship—and how even back then, we southerners were already a mixed tribe with no purity. According to *23 and Me*, my own DNA shows that I'm a soup too—a little African blood, a little Native American, and way back, about 4 percent Neanderthal sprinkled in to spice things up even more.

Thinking about sex and breeding this way, *Mandingo* comes to mind, and the complex, meaningless, and impossible to understand nineteenth-century southern social calculus of octoroon, quadroon, and quintroon. And then there's the way Faulkner juxtaposes the fox released from a crate and run by hounds through Uncle Buck and Buddy's house with the escape of the mixed blood Tomey's Turl in *Go Down, Moses.*

"I've heard this talk before," several of my friends said when I riffed on the idea of red wolves' and coyotes' site-specific consorting then bearing viable young in the distant pocosin swamps of North Carolina.

I don't exactly understand the obsession with purity, with people or wolves. The title of an article Jan wrote in 1992 for the *New York Times* was "Could the Red Wolf be a Mutt?" In the piece she wonders if the federal government had spent twenty years and hundreds of thousands of dollars to preserve a wild mutt? I understand the political complexity of the issue (should the endangered species act protect hybrids?) but I guess I just don't see the depth of the loss if coyotes are successful over the entire South.

Some scientists have even suggested that anxiety over species purity has even affected the way we see nature. If you believe the red wolf is a species then extinction is what we are trying to hold back with the coyote–wolf DMZ, and extinction is a serious issue, or if you believe the red wolf either never existed as a separate species or disappeared centuries or decades ago through interbreeding, then the whole narrative changes and we all must ask a different question such as, "What would be wrong with a landscape filled with successful mutts?"

The tourist trail runs along a ditch for about half a mile, then it intersects with another series of dirt roads that provides access to the crop fields. After the half mile it opens up and you can see a great distance over agricultural fields that over the fall and winter have been flooded. The air was full of the odor of the mud as the fields are drained. I stopped there and the scene took me. Those huge fields are used for growing plants for migrating wildfowl. There were wimbrels working the flats, and their haunting cries punctuated the passing jets performing practice bombing runs just south of us at the Dare County bombing range. The sky was khaki gray and I was transfixed by the intersections around me—animals leaving their signs, the shorebirds working the fecund mud, and the jets above. "If a landscape could be called a mutt, this would be it," I said out loud as the jets passed over.

Betsy walked ahead of me, and when I realized she was out of sight, I took off like one of those fighter jets after her. I had a moment of panic, thinking of my wife's being in "wolf and bear country" alone, but when I came around a curve in the road I saw her ahead walking back toward me smiling. For a moment I was suspended in pure wildness, and I remembered the love of this feeling that I shared with Jan and all others who love the wild. Is that feeling diminished now that there is good evidence that these wolves are proven hybrids? I don't think so. Something is lost, that's for sure, something that Jan gets at in her work. But is everything lost? I hoped silently to myself that the road was clear into the distance for the red wolves, but I had my doubts. The future looks a lot more gray to me than the stark black (coyote) and white (wolf) lines the biologists want to draw in the sand there at Alligator River.

Epilogue MOURNING SONG

"She would of been a good woman," the Misfit said, "if it
had been somebody there to shoot her every minute of her life."
—Flannery O'Connor, "A Good Man Is Hard to Find"

Two years ago, I helped students construct a shack for use
with Wofford College's environmental studies outreach program.
The structure was modeled on Aldo Leopold's old, iconic shack in
Wisconsin.

Conservationist Leopold once described how in "Thinking Like
a Mountain" he saw a "fierce green fire" leaving the eyes of a dying
Mexican gray wolf in southern Arizona. Composed in Wisconsin as
part of an early draft of what would in 1949 become *A Sand County
Almanac*, Leopold's essay outlines a brief scene he remembers taking
place in the mountains of the West decades before. Leopold describes
it as a time "full of trigger-itch," and says in the brief piece, "In those
days we never heard of passing up a chance to kill a wolf." As the
famous scene unfolds, Leopold and his colleagues eat lunch on the
rimrock and see below what they think is a deer wading a stream.
Realizing it's a wolf returning to a den, they start "pumping lead into
the pack" from above, then run down the slope to finish the job.

When I first read Leopold I felt that in the remembered descrip-
tion of killing the wolves he had an elevated view of humans: Leopold
and his friends shot "with more excitement than accuracy," and he
reminded me as a reader that "to aim a steep downhill shot is always
confusing."

For some critics the essay and its powerful rhetoric is an early conservation fable about the role wolves play to keep deer populations in check, of how wolves can stand in as metaphors of wholeness and natural beauty in a landscape; for others it's Leopold's confession of the mistakes he made along the way, a story of awakening, one that others may use for their own enlightenment.

Reading Leopold's "Thinking Like a Mountain" I always reflect back on a scene in Cormac McCarthy's *Cities of the Plain* where the cowboys John Grady Cole and Billy Parham eat their lunch on a ridge and see a single coyote trot out in broad daylight, paying no attention to the men. Their reaction is both similar and more complex than Leopold's.

"I want you to look at that son of a bitch," Billy says as the coyote emerges from the brush and trots along the ridge, on the same level as the two cowboys.

John Grady goes for his rifle and almost takes a long unlikely shot. Billy discourages him, saying the coyote will "be gone before you get done standin up."

"You think he seen us?" John Grady asks.

Billy answers, "I don't expect he was completely blind."

I focus on the connection to the eyes here, of the coyote watching the two cowboys, just out of range. The wolf that Leopold and his trigger-happy friends fill with lead is unaware of the danger until it's too late. This could be read as a parable about wolves and coyotes and their hope for survival as a species, a parable playing out now in the Southeast. Though adaptable, wolves are often so wild that they need wilderness to survive. They've been called an indicator species of wildness in that way. The coyote in McCarthy's narrative is a survivor. His kind don't need as much. The cowboys are blind to the coyote's presence until it wanders out into the daylight and glances their way. John Grady Cole does not shoot. As the scene ends the coyote trots along the ridge and stops to look back, then drops off down the ridge into the brush below. In Leopold's story the humans descend on the she-wolf in time to see the last of her wild world burning away in a green haze. In McCarthy's fable the fire is banked with coals behind the distant coyote eyes. Even if a green fire does burn, the cowboys will never get close enough to see it.

When finished, I imagined our Leopold outreach shack brimming with pelts, skulls, nests, shells, husks, bones, fossils, and rocks like an old-timey scout hut or that trapper's cabin in *The Crossing*, an alternative to the direction science education has been headed for thirty years. Instead of sitting in air-conditioned rooms and scanning screens or crunching numbers, the young would put their hands on the leftover or discarded materials of the world and discover the local landscape firsthand in order to utilize it in some magical way.

Because there is still a fairly abundant population of common mammals in the upcountry of South Carolina it was easy to get study material for the shack. For the shack project, I enlisted Mike Willis as a sort of odd college adjunct—the Aldo Leopold Professor of Roadkill and Nuisance Trapping.

Besides Mike's help, an unexpected source of skins came from a local wildlife officer, who got wind of our educational project, liked the sound of it, and said that he would contribute animals when he could. Within a month of our beginning to gather specimens, the officer called and explained he had a dead coyote.

"Bring it on down," I said. "We'll throw it in the Goodall Center's freezer and skin it out later for the shack."

Whether I like it or not, the coyote in South Carolina falls under the "vermin" category and is offered very little protection. When the officer arrived with the carcass he told me the sad story of the coyote's demise. An anonymous tip had directed him to Craigslist, where a local man was trying to sell a live coyote for a hundred dollars, an illegal act under wildlife laws in South Carolina.

Our local wildlife officer tracked down the man's address, arrived at his trailer, wrote the man up, and confiscated the injured emaciated animal from a pen in the man's backyard. By state law the coyote could not be transported or relocated, so my future coyote pelt, a young skinny male, had a bullet hole in the skull when it arrived, and that bullet hole prompted me to return to the image that had birthed this narrative: Leopold's fierce green fire leaving a dying canid's eyes in New Mexico almost a hundred years earlier. Was my pelt project a way to carry out Leopold's conservation of predators in South Carolina? I don't know what Aldo Leopold would have had to say about coyotes coming into the South. He had plenty to say about "invasive species," if that's what coyotes can be called. Wildlife ecologists Stan Temple and Christopher Bocast have noted how the "soundscape" of Leopold's Sand County has changed as exotic species have moved in since Leopold's time and occupied the countryside, and how Leopold believed listening to the sounds of a place can give you an indication of the place's health. This made me think about coyote sounds behind my house and how hopeful I find them. Would Aldo Leopold listen to them and hear health and redemption, or disease, disruption, and degradation?

I'd never skinned out a coyote and I didn't want to spoil our first specimen. Mike Willis said he'd skin it out, and then we'd take it to a tannery over in Greenville "run by a Russian." Our dead coyote would become a pelt, or as the professor in me preferred, "a study skin."

I'd just gotten back from a college up north where I'd talked publicly about my coyote project. I'd read four poems about animals, and then I'd read the opening to my book. A woman in the audience didn't quite get my thesis, that having coyotes around might just be a good thing. She asked, "Why do humans need a top-of-the-food-chain predator around, and why can't we just get along without one around here in the East as we have for one hundred and fifty years?"

It was a good question if you like security, since this newly arrived predator is killing our cats and dogs and even occasionally threatening our children, and I didn't have a pat answer. I said I believed that the coming of the coyotes might just end up being our savior from an overpopulation of deer, and then I added, "You know, a single coyote can kill and eat thousands of mice in a year too. That's a thousand good reasons to have them around."

Another woman in the audience followed up: "We've been out of that natural food chain so long. Why do we have to jump back into it?"

"We really aren't removed from the food chain," I said. "It's just that the dirty work is done for us by meat processors. A friend of mine who is a hunter once said, 'If you want to get sentimental about the death of mammals, just start with your own shoes and belts.'"

The tannery Mike knew about operates deep in the industrial ruin of Poinsett Highway in the shadow of one of Greenville, South Carolina's, old textile mills—a gray concrete-block building with no windows and a lock on the door. In March on the way to Alabama we stopped to drop off the coyote pelt and some other roadkill skins Mike had gathered for the shack. We buzzed to get in. A skinny young man opened up. He'd been working at a long bloody bench scraping the fat and flesh off fresh hides. He wasn't happy to see us. After the young man let us in, he walked back to the bench and continued, stripping and cutting at hide after hide, and throwing slices of meat into a trashcan. He glanced down at Mike's plastic bags full of skins and asked, "Do you skin 'em or do you just jerk 'em off, meat and all?"

"No, I skin 'em," Mike answered.

The young man unzipped one of the bags and inspected Mike's skins, zipped the bag shut again, and laid it on the metal table. "He'll check you in back there," the young man said, pointing with his bloody knife to a tall, stocky presence prowling among the pallets of processed pelts at the back of the building like a foraging bear. I assumed this was Mike's "Russian."

"What a nightmare," I thought at first glance, but then I became interested in the tannery in the way you can become fascinated with a wreck on the side of the highway.

"How many tanneries are there in the upstate?" I asked Mike.

"This just might be the only one," he said.

Mike introduced himself, and I quickly heard why he called the man the Russian. His thick accent sounded like something out of a B-grade spy film, but it didn't seem to slow him down from talking. He jabbered on in workmanlike lists as he sorted through Mike's pelts—"two beaver, gray fox, red fox, raccoon, mink, and one coyote." Mike introduced me, and I shook the Russian's hand. His fingers were square, squat, and wet from all the hides he'd been handling.

Mike asked the Russian if he bought deer hides, and instead of answering, the Russian explained something I'd finally been able to follow, how the Plains Indian tribes prefer southeastern deer fur to northeastern deer fur to make their tourist items because it's shorter, and fly fishermen want to use the northern hair to tie flies. He never exactly answered Mike's question, but I assumed the story confirmed that, yes, he needed deerskins.

As Mike talked with the Russian, I looked around more. The tannery was cluttered. How did the Russian keep up with anything? Small tags identified each of the hides ready for pickup, but the tanned hides were piled everywhere, in all open spaces. There were thousands of skins and a great deal of variety—I could recognize deer, bear, bobcat, coyote, beaver, hundreds of raccoons. There were also exotic animals such as zebra, buffalo, even wolves.

In a back corner of the building I watched as a gray-haired woman fed hides into three huge rotating drums, mixing them with sawdust. The process smelled fleshy, and the machines roared like industrial dryers as they tumbled. It wasn't a bad smell. "A little leathery," Mike said when I commented on the odor. Mike sensed what I was feeling and tried to calm me. "I'll bet this is rough on you."

"I'm OK," I said, but it was hard for me to see those thousands of animal hides tanned and waiting in stacks in the building to be shipped out to God knows where.

Besides us, there were three other men wandering around the place as well, and Mike struck up a conversation with them. They were taxidermists from Spartanburg. One pulled out his cell phone and flipped through pictures of a series of big dead deer for Mike to see. "They're high-fence deer from Kentucky," Mike turned and explained what I was seeing, in case I didn't understand. The man flipped through to a particular deer with ornate antlers and said, "It cost twenty-five thousand dollars to shoot that one."

"Damn," the other man exclaimed. "You could get a bass boat for that."

A single human life has its joys, triumphs, and disappointments, which environmentalists can tend to undervalue, either for the good or bad of it. Sometimes the future emerges in single lives in ways we can't control or imagine—illnesses, the arrival of love or the failure to find love, etc.—and then some of life's possibility and reward just stubs out. It's not all "systems thinking," or what the poet Gary Snyder calls "being in line with the big flow." Sometimes it's just the day-to-day and other "developments"— psychological, biological, social, religious, political, and historical. How to sustain a single human life? That's part of the paradox too, isn't it? But then is the same not true with all living things? Not just *Homo sapiens*?

Coyotes are out there living day to day, always with death right beside them, over the ridge, or down the road. As the Flannery O'Connor quotation points out, the proximity to death might be just what makes us good. If that's true, then coyotes are one of the best animals we've got because there is somebody or something there to kill them every minute of their lives—mange, heartworm, cars, hunters, and trappers.

Of course, that begs the question, what is good? Why are coyotes good? Why are they called vermin? More and more as I worked on this book I realized that my story is about how they are living "among" us. How will it be that we carry on in that relationship to them for generations, for centuries? We humans are trained to never give up on anything, so how could I expect my neighbors and fellow southerners to cede that hard-won cultural territory—the backyard, the neighborhood, the city block, the farm field, the hunting lease, to another creature as territory? But can they teach us about survival as a species?

I care about distant species where we control their destiny, like wolves or elephants or rhinos, but I'm more interested in the ones, close by, who seem to be traveling with us—crows, bears, mice, and of course, these coyotes. I like to follow the lives of the animal presences that flourish in the margins we have created. I know it's going to be tough to ask these questions. There's a lot of coyote hate out there, and the coyote fear is building as well. I started talking about this recently with a friend. He'd killed a ten-point buck. Like the taxidermists in the tannery, he clicked through pictures on his cell. He had shots of a dead coyote. He'd shot it. He'd taken a close up of the coyote's head with its big white fangs. (He called them fangs.) "They're hell on deer fawns," he said. "I wish somebody would show me how to kill 'em all and I would."

I asked him about his other experiences with coyotes, and he said in all his time in a tree stand he'd only seen two, and this was the first he'd shot. "They don't respond to 'calling up' the way foxes do. You can play that fox-calling tape and foxes will come right up to the truck and you can shoot them right there next to it, but not a coyote. We never see them, though we do hear 'em and then they'll be gone for months. I guess they're just passing through."

He paused, flipped back through the pictures, then said, "When I was hunting I saw a small buck come out of the woods, and as the buck walked along he kept looking back, and as I tracked him in my scope I saw coming out of the woods this big coyote trailing the deer." At first he'd thought it was a big bobcat; "Then I thought it was a dog," he said. "I got a bead on him and saw it was a coyote. I dropped him right there. It was a big male. He had a perfect coat except for that bullet hole."

In her book *The Old Way* Elizabeth Marshall Thomas writes about the age-old realities of human–animal relations. Thomas recounts her time as a teen with the Bushmen in southern Africa in a not-so-distant and imaginable past. What could this book about Africa teach me about coyotes coming into the South? The first chapter is all about the "Old Way" the Bushmen came out of when Thomas spent years with them in the 1950s with her family, how that way of life at that time was mostly unchanged since the Pleistocene, and how our species, living that Old Way, was just a species among species. She used an analogy first presented by Richard Dawkins of a line of people holding hands, generation by generation, all the way back to the dawn of the species until that first *Homo sapiens* clasps the hand of an ape ancestor.

Thomas pushes it a little further. She has us holding hands all the way back through the other species in our line. We are all animals holding hands (or paws), and we were all part of the Old Way, at least until the end of the Neolithic when humans began to separate ourselves from the other animals.

Thomas does not apologize for her anthropomorphic comparisons, and neither do I. When I cast my imagination out into our floodplain, it's not exactly anthropomorphizing I'm up to. I call it kin recognition, attending to a family reunion, communing with my mammal cousins, distant and even troublesome, but not easily forgotten. I share close to 75 percent of my DNA with these canines, so what I see in a coyote's eyes can't be attributed to hunger alone, no more than it could if I looked into my own eyes in a mirror.

Thomas believes you can talk about all animals living in the Old Way with the same anthropological terms such as family, generations, and community. "For those who live in the Old Way certain elements never vary. Your group size is set by the food supply, your territory must include water, the animals you hunt will always be afraid of you, and the plant foods will always be seasonal, so you had better remember where they grow and be there when they are fruiting." Thomas reflects beautifully on how we as a species were shaped because of climate change and how we adapted to the changes. "Small and light bodied, deft and graceful, these very successful people stayed in the places that shaped our species, living in the Old Way, with aspects of the culture such as group size, ways of gathering foods, and territorial requirements very similar to those of many other creatures, all shaped by necessity in a manner that most of us today cannot imagine."

Reading Thomas I thought about the remarkable range extension of the coyote and what our anthropocentric land use change has meant to them as a species. In just one hundred years they've evolved from a twenty-five-pound canine species, restricted to the West and Midwest mostly, to a species now covering all of North America. In some places they've mated with wolves and dogs along their journey, and their genes and those genes are intermingled forever now, making them bigger and better hunters of larger game, but also creating the perfect omnivore, even better I'd say than we or the bears are, because of their smaller size and their stealth. Now they have settled a region with abundant water and an endless supply of food (both wild and human), good cover for dens, and changing attitudes about hunting and trapping that make it difficult to imagine the world without them. "Our creator was the ice age," Thomas says. And the creator of the new coyote has been us and maybe the age of us, what some have begun calling the Anthropocene.

Maybe in the five or so generations that coyotes have been in the South they have even developed what we might call a social fabric. Maybe they have figured out ways to cope with the high mortality of their family groups through hunting and trapping, heartworms, distemper, and roadkill, and that there is a certain cautious comfort to their lives foraging, hunting, and seasonally mating.

Though we hear them often, we see coyotes mostly by chance or dead on the side of the road. We don't often get to see them being coyotes, and when we do (with the now ubiquitous game cameras) we often misinterpret what they are doing. Though I have spent hours in the woods, I have not observed wild coyotes for more than a few seconds—four times to be exact—each time as an individual walked away from me on a trail or stood on the roadside as I passed in my truck. I have thought about them enough and wondered what they are thinking about us. We are told that coyotes must fear humans if we are going to live together. That's probably true. Lines need to be drawn between species. Even Elizabeth Marshall Thomas describes the Bushmen shaking a burning branch at the lions on the edge of their camp and saying in a loud, firm voice, "Old lions, you can't be here. If you come nearer we will hurt you. So go now. Go!"

This said, researchers know a great deal about coyotes, but they don't know for sure what is maybe the essential thing for us to know. They don't know yet how coyotes are changing and will continue to change to adapt to this new place and how those changes will affect both us and the coyotes over time.

I'm beginning to form a mental picture of a web of familiar relations covering the South, coyote mothers, fathers, daughters, and sons, aunts and uncles, nieces and nephews, coyote family circles within coyote family circles, stretching from the Mason-Dixon Line to the tip of the Florida Keys, from the coastal sea islands to the Mississippi River. The hunters and the trappers, the diseases and the speeding cars, all gnaw at the edges of these circles but do not disperse them, and the natural history of the continent would suggest they will not. Just as the pioneers and hunters and government trappers attempted to eradicate the coyotes out west for one hundred years, so the southerners hold such dreams. But the coyote will prevail. That's my theory and I'm sticking to it. They will be living here as long as we will, their dens and fairways and hunting trails as permanent as our suburbs and interstates.

In a recent article in *National Geographic* Douglas Chadwick lays out the case of cougars expanding back into their extensive former range. For the moment the cougar is still found mostly west of the Mississippi (with the exception of a small population in south Florida), but the highly adaptable cats are extending their range. The big cats have "spilled eastward" across the upper Great Plains and even across the top of the Great Lakes. There have been reports of cats the biologists refer to as "wayfarers" wandering as far as the Northeast. In 2011 a young male was hit by an suv in Connecticut, and genetic tests revealed the cat came from the Black Hills of South Dakota. Was that young cat out for a two-thousand-mile walkabout, or was he an advance scout paving the way for the long-run expansion?

Jim Sterba in *Nature Wars* makes a convincing argument for the comeback in the East of five native species eradicated in the last century: beavers, deer, geese, turkeys, and black bears. Cougars seem on the same trajectory. This was possible primarily because we in the East once more live in the midst of a great forest, offering plenty of habitats for all creatures great and small, for prey and predators. Of our wild neighbors, Sterba says, "More are on the way, moving in among us as their populations thrive and spread . . . in some cases far beyond their historic ranges." Sterba isn't hopeful about the future of our interactions with wildlife: "This is a new way of living for both human and beast, and Americans haven't figured out how to do it. . . . Americans have become denatured." We, he argues, don't have the skills to manage "an often unruly natural world."

I'll admit that even I am a little queasy about this "unruly natural world" that Sterba announces. Every night when I let Murphy out into the fenced backyard, I fret that he will have an unexpected encounter with the wild, particularly that family group of coyotes calling the floodplain home. The coyotes are out there. Being wild, in shape, and honed to a sharp point of aggression by life in the near-woods, they would make quick business of Murphy, my short-legged couch beagle. If the coyotes did attack they would have little trouble jumping the fence and running him down, and I don't think Murphy would put up much of a fight.

Maybe I should let Murphy out and then follow his strong nose to the edge of the yard and take a sniff myself. Maybe I should yell into the darkness, like a Deep South bushman, or Derrick Jensen, "Coyotes, please leave my beagle alone. If you do this I promise I will follow suggestions to keep my dog safe from you including keeping noise-makers like whistles and horns on hand to scare you away if you enter my yard, not turning my back on you, not allowing you get in between me and Murphy, and finally I will work as a writer to teach people to understand your species better."

But it may be too late to add rules to my backyard. A map in the *National Geographic* cougar article looks eerily like the coyote map of range expansion in Gerry Parker's coyote book. There are dark areas delineating the present "cougar comeback," and then there are four or five arrows pointing out possible dispersal routes to new territory. One dark arrow in particular leaves South Dakota and picks up another arrow arching across the Great Lakes and into the Northeast.

Unlike Sterba, *National Geographic*'s Chadwick doesn't hold back his excitement about the expansion of wild creatures like cougars into territories they haven't occupied in a hundred years. "It seems vital to many people that something big and fierce is out there wilding the landscape," he says, "something that prickles the hair on the back of the neck and fires the imagination."

But what does this wilding of the landscape mean for all the other folk, the vast majority of southern *Homo sapiens* who also share the territories but are unprepared for this new way of living? Sometimes when I'm feeling my most apocalyptic I imagine a distant future in which these "denatured" southerners look up and notice for the first time that the woodlands and wetlands surrounding them are popu-lated with coyotes yipping at sirens, black bears raiding the bird feed-ers, and even cougars caught on game cams. (And to add one more nightmare scenario, the pythons might, by that time, have made it all the way to the Georgia line, drainage ditch by drainage ditch.)

By that time the current downward trend in southern hunters will have made it unlikely to control these large mammals from tree stands or with traps. There will be no solution short of bringing in the National Guard as they did in West Virginia with the outlaw coyote.

The general population—obese, unaware, untrained in natural history, much less yard maintenance—won't notice the change until it's too late and they're trapped indoors thumbing their remote controls and adjusting their air conditioning. The coyotes and bears and cougars won't be using remote controls. They'll be settled in, operating on instincts and native intelligence, paws on the ground, checking out what opportunities the new neighborhood offers. Cowered in their midcentury modern dens in aging suburbs backing up to greenways, undeveloped parkland, remnant agricultural land, and railroad right-of-ways, the denatured *Homo sapiens* will fear (and rightly so) for their poodles, their bird feeders, maybe even their children on the rare instance the young wander out of the monitor's shadow. In my vision, most southerners will be prisoners to the wild.

We picked up our furs a few months later in Greenville. The same young man still stood carving the meat off raw skins at the front table, and when we wandered in, he didn't even look up. The Russian recognized us and greeted us from the back loading dock, stacked chest high with raccoon pelts. He wiped his hands on a spare towel, shook Mike's, then mine. Mike explained we were here to pick up an order for Willis, and the Russian looked through a nearby canvas cart full of finished furs until he came to what he was looking for, a plastic band looped through the finished furs with Mike's name on it. We followed the Russian to his front office where he laid the string of multicolored mammal furs before him and then sat behind an old desk to fill out a bill of sale. We waited across from him in two leatherette chairs out of proportion with the room. When he finished he handed the bill over to Mike, then the Russian picked up each finished fur and held them in his hands, showing pride in his work. The red fox was the most remarkable, the depth of color and thickness of the orange-red fur was so exorbitant in its tint, though the gray fox was a close second; but that was my assessment before I had seen the two beaver furs and the mink; they were by far the most striking. I couldn't believe how thick and luxuriant the brown fur seemed and couldn't wait until the Russian handed them over and I could run my fingers through them as well. In that instant I felt great pride. I saw and felt why furs like this had once been so valuable as a cash crop and how whole economies had once risen and fallen on their availability. I knew that in Mike's past life as a trapper he'd seen thousands of these furs, but I felt like he still got a charge out of seeing them across the table, fully realized in their beauty and depth of value.

The coyote fur was on the bottom, the last the Russian picked up. The gray fur of that emaciated, captive animal was thin but I remember thinking that the pelt was still beautiful, a fitting tribute to one dead coyote in the upcountry of South Carolina. "This is a good coyote," I thought, bringing to mind Flannery O'Connor's quote. With this tanning process we'd created an afterlife of a sort for at least this animal, and we'd also fostered sympathy, as J. Frank Dobie had urged in his book *The Voice of the Coyote*, that always derives from knowledge and understanding. Our coyote would live on in our outreach shack and work hard for environmental education for years to come. Little kids would hold the pelt and know what coyote fur felt like. This coyote wasn't Scooter, a live presence before them, but he was something.

The Russian knew none of this as he rubbed the pelt between his thumb and forefinger to show us how thin. "It poor skin," he said, shaking his head. "No use to anybody." But I knew a younger generation would learn from the stories told around this coyote. They would know the coyotes live among us, how they are omnivores and eat as much fruit and they do meat, how they are secretive and resilient and resourceful, how people are unjustly cruel to them, and their suffering is often out of proportion to their transgressions, and how we must learn to manage our relationships with them and not act out of ignorance and fear the way we had for two hundred years out west. This skin would help close the gap between reality and myth in our small corner of the South.

As one last departing customer service, the Russian placed all the furs in a plastic bag and handed them across the table to Mike. I picked up the bill, looked at the price. I added up the number of skins and multiplied by what Mike had told me earlier they'd cost. The Russian had charged me $140 for two beavers, the red and gray fox, the mink, two otters, and the coyote. I paid in cash, but I noted the total was $20 less than I expected. I thought maybe he'd added wrong, and before I left I asked the Russian about the low price. "No problem," he said and smiled. "I throw in coyote for free."

Acknowledgments

A longer version of the prologue "Redemption Song" appeared in *Earthlines: The Culture of Nature* (no. 3, November 2012, Isle of Lewis, Outer Hebrides) and "Scatology" appeared originally in *Ecotone* (no. 15, 2013, University of North Carolina–Wilmington); many thanks to Sharon Blackie (*Earthlines*) and David Gessner (*Ecotone*) for showing support for this project from an early stage by publishing these essays.

Also, I thank these good readers and listeners among my larger writing community: Barry Lopez, Rick Bass, Bronwen Dickey, Kurt Caswell, Catherine Reid, Curt Meine, Josephine Humphreys, Hal Herzog, John Kilgo, Rhett Johnson, Phil Wilkinson, Ab Abercrombie, Gerald Thurmond, Terry Ferguson, Kaye Savage, Peter Brewitt, Vivian Fisher, G. R. Davis, John Mohler, John Simmons, George Tyson, and Johnny Stowe. More thanks than I can express go to Mike Willis for showing me the piedmont Old Way and traveling with me in search of Señor Coyote with a distinctive southern accent; and to Drew Lanham, poet, hunter, ornithologist, master teacher of wildlife classes, song-dog champion, and great literary friend, who listened, read, and reacted to so much of this book in real time through Instant Messenger, texts, and e-mail and phone; and finally, as always, I would like to thank my wife, Betsy, the best support a writer could have, who tuned my ear to the floodplain and always encouraged me to move the real coyotes to the front of the story. And finally, a big thank you, as well, goes out to the good folks at the University of Georgia Press for support, preparation, and publication of this book—James Patrick Allen for acquiring this project, Sue Breckenridge for copyediting, and also to David Des Jardines, Jon Davies, and the design staff for, as always, doing great work.

Notes

Below, listed chapter by chapter, are works referred to in the text, some that contributed facts, and others that influenced my ideas about coyotes coming into the South.

Prologue: Redemption Song

The most extensive review of eastern and southern coyote research to date is "Coyote (*Canis latrans*), 100+ Years in the East: A Literature Review," by Lauren L. Mastro, Eric M. Gese, Julie K. Young, and John A. Shivik, which was presented at the Fourteenth Wildlife Damage Management Conference in 2012. The compilers presented this as a "comprehensive review of the existing literature to illuminate the gaps in our knowledge that can be used to direct future research." The paper "illuminated deficiencies in the quality and quantity of information in all areas of eastern coyote ecology." It is important that this be kept in mind as you read my explorations into the lives and myths of this elusive animal.

"There have been dozens of coyote attacks and at least one death . . ." In 2009 a nineteen-year-old folk singer was hiking alone in Nova Scotia when she was attacked and killed by a pack of coyotes. There have been hundreds of reported coyote bites in the United States since 1960, mostly in the western and northeastern United States.

Scatology

"Scatology" first appeared in the journal *Ecotone*, and its founding editor, David Gessner wrote of Cape Cod coyotes in his collection *Sick of Nature*, published in 2004. It is from David some of the inspiration for this collection arose, and his piece, "Howling with the Trickster: A Wild Memoir," is still one of the most interesting and challenging accounts of coyote coming east.

Coyote on the Run

"When Richard first told me of his latest hunting research . . ." Richard Rankin recently published a book of essays, *Margins of a Greater Wildness*, which offers his own compelling account of a similar hilltop hunt and the traditions it encompasses.

"The larger cultural context of hilltop fox chasing . . ." Tad Sitton's *Gray Ghosts and Red Rangers* (2010) is full of primary accounts from fox hunting publications such as *Hunters Horn*, and it forms a remarkable social history of hilltopping. By the end of Sitton's account I was convinced, as Sitton had been, that the passing of this hunting form is the loss of an "ancient ritual," and that we are smaller for its loss. The full final paragraph of the book is worth repeating here in its entirety: "What kind of deep play was Hilltopping, what cultural message did it assert, what story did playing its game tell hunters about themselves? Certainly it asserted the persistence of wilderness and wilderness ways, including the rights of hunters, hounds, and foxes to range far and wide across the countryside in the freedom of the chase. Against the rising tide of modernity, fences, and Posted signs it asserted hunters' rights, the free range, and open woods and the boisterous cry of the pack crossing private land carried a faintly implied treat. For the people who practiced it, hilltopping told that men are beasts as well as men; that men are natural hunters, akin to hounds; that hunters compete with other hunters for scarce resources; and that, in the rigor of this competition, men and hounds (and their remarkable quarry) share certain ultimate virtues of bravery, endurance, determination, honor, beauty, story-telling, and music."

"It goes back to Faulkner . . ." The best introduction to the hunting stories of Faulkner is to read all the works and search them out, but if you do not have time to do that, track down an important edited collection called *Big Woods: The Hunting Stories of William Faulkner* (1955) with remarkable "decorations" by Edward Shenton. The collection includes a shorter version of "The Bear," "The Old People," "A Bear Hunt," and "Race at Morning." It was Faulkner who added the italicized comments before each story, and they are worth the effort to find the book; in the first one he describes southern wilderness as well as it has ever been rendered: "One jungle one brake one impassable density of brier and cane and vine interlocking the soar of gum and cypress and hickory and pin oak and ash, printed now by the tracks of unalien shapes—bear and deer and panthers and wolves and alligators and the myriad smaller beasts." And to this litany now we can add coyotes.

Coyote Hugger

"In a more contemporary tale, Barry Lopez explains . . ." Barry Lopez's *Of Wolves and Men* (1978) is an important text that stands behind my own explorations of the animal world that includes our own species. The powerful epilogue speaks most clearly to the relationships among wolves, coyotes, and humans, and in the beginning of the last paragraph Lopez makes clear his motivation for such a study: "It is with this freedom from dogma, I imagine, that the meaning of the words 'the celebration of life' becomes clear."

Scooter is now in his third year as an outreach animal and his story can be found at http://srel.uga.edu/outreach/animals/coyote.htm. Since my visit in 2014 Sean Poppy reports, "Scooter is doing well. He continues to be cooperative at presentations and is now consuming his first roadkill hog. In October he battled with some dogs (neighbor's?) through his fence and injured himself. Instead of trapping/shooting the dogs, I put up a shorter perimeter fence outside of his to prevent animals from getting close to him and that seems to be working."

Beyond the Reach of the Loudspeakers

John Kilgo, et al., "Can Coyotes Affect Deer Populations in Southeastern North America?," *Journal of Wildlife Management* 74, no. 5 (2010): 929–33; DOI: 10.2193/2009-263. This is one of many articles about fawn predation. Worth a read if you want to understand the complexity of the deer/coyote issue in the South!

"Though coyotes killing an adult deer in the South is probably a rare thing . . ." Near completion of this book an article appeared in *Notes of the*

Southeastern Naturalist (13, no. 3 [2014]) by M. Colter Chitwood, Marcus A. Lashley, Christopher E. Moorman, and Christopher S. DePermo describing what may be the first scientific reports of coyotes killing adult deer in the South. The brief report, called "Confirmation of Coyote Predation on Adult Female White-Tailed Deer in the Southeastern United States," outlines research conducted at Fort Bragg, in eastern North Carolina. The descriptions of the deaths tracks closely with what I imagine: "Two females left noticeable blood trails and trampled vegetation, which indicated prolonged struggle."

"As early as the 1990s researchers in Alabama, Kentucky, Mississippi, and Tennessee . . ." In the bibliography I list a few of these key papers if you are interested in pursuing this any further.

Outlaw Coyote

"Lives of animals are good to use to think about our own lives . . ." Editors Angus K. Gillespie and Jay Mechling develop this idea at some length in the introduction to *American Wildlife in Symbol and Story*.

"Right in the middle of the lobby stands a mount of the maverick coyote . . ." I first became aware of the story of the outlaw coyote after reading a footnote in Gerry Parker's book, *Eastern Coyote: The Story of Its Success*.

"A few years later, in 1993, Jordan Fisher Smith conducted an interview with Wendell Berry . . ." Jordan Fisher Smith's interview is called "Field Observations: An Interview with Wendell Berry" and can be found on the envirolinks website: http://arts.envirolink.org/interviews_and_conversations /WendellBerry.html.

Coyote under the Pear Tree

Kingsolver's novel *Prodigal Summer* (2000) was published to mixed reviews. Reviewers complained about the long, complex discussions about ecology and ecosystems and predators that Deanna and Eddie Bondo have between heated bouts of sex. "Biology may be destiny in the forest," Jennifer Schuessler wrote in the *New York Times Review of Books*, "but good fiction—like good sex— happens mostly in the head." Much was made of Kingsolver's dissertations about the natural world and how they overpowered the narrative. This is what attracts me to the story. Even if Deanne's discussions fall flat as fiction, the narrative is certainly compelling as a source for ideas about coyotes coming into the South. Kingsolver is a fine biologist as well as novelist.

"A good thing to have a predator, a 'carnivore,' back at the top of the food chain . . ." Eddie Bondo calls the coyote a "carnivore" and yet most place the animals in the omnivore family. Some biologists, like Henry Hilton in "Systematics and Ecology of the Eastern Coyote," call the coyote "versatile" and "opportunistic." Others, like Gerry Parker, in *Eastern Coyote*, go a step further, saying the coyote is "efficient . . . a predator . . . a generalist." If the coyote is indeed, like us (and the crows, the bears, and the sparrows) an omnivore, then our dilemma will always be not what to eat (everything), but where to find enough.

Byford's article is about coyote foodways, called "Coyotes Are Not Finicky Eaters" in the December 15, 2004, issue of the newsletter *Southeast Farm Press*. I like Byford's tone as much as anything I encountered in my research about coyotes. He's funny yet serious and practical at the same time. He says, "Livestock producers blame [coyotes] for killing calves, lambs, and kids. Quail and rabbit hunters blame them for less game to hunt. Others say coyotes have killed out all the ground hogs. . . . (So far I haven't heard them blamed for hurricanes, downturn in the stock market, or hordes of blackbirds.) . . . It's not my purpose to protect coyotes or vilify them. I'm just trying to set the record straight."

In the spiraling way that research for this book progressed, I was reading about beaver trapping in *A Savage Empire* (2011) by Alan Axelrod, and I came across his well-articulated debunking of myth about the differences between early English trappers and French trappers: that it's not so simple that the French earned the beaver trade with Native Americans through friendship through extensive intermarrying and that the English viewed them as inferiors. He calls this both "anachronistic and simplistic." It's anachronistic because "it's founded on our own assumptions about racial perception and identification rather than on the beliefs and behavior" of the time. The simplicity comes from not adequately "accounting for all the motives of the players of that same time and place." So Axelrod helped spawn this metaphor of "Fort Apache and a French trading post." Maybe I'm pushing way too far (and ruining a perfectly good metaphor) by connecting the coyote book backward in time to the early trade wars in North America, but I don't think so. The coming of the coyotes into the South is a little like our invasion of North America and our establishment of the *Homo sapiens* lifeway from sea to shining sea. Maybe we need to find a way to account for "all the motives of the players" of this current settlement drama to get it right. Could it be a vast simplification to reduce the motives of coyotes to food and sex?

David George Haskell's *The Forest Unseen: A Year's Watch in Nature* (2012) was published to great acclaim. It was a finalist for the Pulitzer Prize and won a handful of other awards. Haskell's poetic language and use of metaphor verges on the literary, and his image of the coyote dancing over the food web is one of the primary touchstones of my thought and reflection on the species. At the end of his epilogue Haskell says, "Part of what we discover by observing ourselves is an affinity for the world around us." This could serve as an epigraph for this book.

"The recessive gene found in southern coyotes picked up somewhere along the species' genetic journey . . ." Black coyotes are rare, and Christopher B. Mowry and Justin L. Edge have researched black (melanistic) coyotes in northwestern Georgia, and in 2014 they published their results in *Southeastern Naturalist*. Their research shows "the ancestry of southeastern coyotes is unclear" and therefore the origin of is still uncertain. Until more research is conducted it may be impossible to point with certainty to the presence of dog and wolf genes as the origin of the black coyotes.

Island Coyote

"In the 1980s there had been a paper by biologists about work on fawn predation . . ." M. B. Epstein, G. A. Feldhamer, R. L. Joyner, R. J. Hamilton, and W. G. Moore, "Home Range and Mortality of White-Tailed Deer Fawns in Coastal South Carolina," *Proceedings of the Annual Conference of Southeastern Association of Fish and Wildlife Agencies* 39 (1985):373–79.

Danny's Field

"There lived a woman named May Jordan . . ." When my friend and Alabama native Vivian Fisher found out I was writing about the piney woods of lower

Alabama, she put me on to May Jordan's journals: *Where the Wild Animals Is Plentiful: Diary of an Alabama Fur Trader's Daughter, 1912–1914*, edited by Elisa Moore Baldwin (Tuscaloosa: University of Alabama Press, 2006).

Suburban Coyote

When I was alerted to the presence of Meredith Doster's blog entry "The Suburban Wild: Coyotes in Druid Hills" on Southern Spaces website in the spring of 2013 I knew that I had stumbled upon the scent trail of a great story about southern coyotes. This has all the elements: the fear, the confusion, the surprise, and the complex solutions fracturing along many intellectual lines.

Those interested can find Meredith's blog at http.//www.southernspaces .org/blog/suburban-wild-coyotes-druid-hills. The video of the Druid Hills coyote meeting that I watched in order to write this chapter can be found on the East Lake Road Neighborhood Association Web Page: http://eastlakeneighborhood .org/full-video-of-the-jan-29-coyote-meeting/.

In Derrick Jenson's *A Language Older than Words* (2000) he urges people "to live in dynamic equilibrium with the rest of the world." *Publishers Weekly* said of it, "His visceral, biting observations always manage to lead back to his mantra: 'Things don't have to be the way they are.'"

Miscegenation

"Since 1994 'genetic swamping' of the red wolf by the influx of coyotes . . ." There is a fairly lengthy discussion of the impact of coyote–red wolf hybridization in the article "Restoration of the Red Wolf" by Michael K. Phillips, V. Gary Henry, and Brian T. Kelly (USDA National Wildlife Research Center Staff Publication, 2003). It is one of the most entertaining of the technical articles about the wolf restoration, as the authors quote from field journals of the scientists on the project and draw a few broad conclusions. They believe it will be necessary to study the extent of "introgression between red wolf and coyote populations" and actively manage them in order to ensure that "coyotes will not again genetically 'swamp' red wolves."

"According to Stephen Jay Gould . . ." Gould carries out this lively discussion of speciation in *Discovery* ("What Is a Species?" December 1992).

"Some scientists have even suggested that anxiety over species purity has even affected the way we see nature." In a short piece published in the *New York Times Sunday Magazine* (August 17, 2014) about what it means to be a species, Moises Velasquez quotes geneticist Michael Arnold: "Anxiety over racial 'purity' perhaps affected the way we thought about nature.... It's sort of cool that evolution is really messy." In this piece Valasquez also discusses the coywolf but doesn't mention the drama at Alligator River.

Epilogue: Mourning Song

"Wildlife ecologists Stan Temple and Christopher Bocast have noted how the 'soundscape' of Leopold's Sand County has changed . . ." For an exciting discussion of this subject see an article by Terry Devitt, "Aldo Leopold's Field Notes Score a Lost 'Soundscape,'" about the work of Temple and Bocast (*University of Wisconsin–Madison News*, September 18, 2012, http://www.news.wisc.edu/21058).

"In a recent article in *National Geographic* Douglas Chadwick..." Chadwick's piece in *National Geographic* (December 2013) is called "Ghost Cats," and in it he surveys the latest intelligence on the cougar comeback.

"Jim Sterba in *Nature Wars* ..." Sterba's fine book is maybe the best popular study out there on the complexities associated with the "rewilding" of the East (and of those who inhabit it) and should be required reading for all interested in this topic.

Resources

The following texts have been added to the shelf beside my writing desk in a less-than-systematic fashion over the course of the last five years composing *Coyote Settles the South*. I have listed them chronologically, in the order they appeared in the world, as in this odd fashion they tell an interesting and evolving story of thinking about animals and, finally, about coyotes moving into the twenty-first century as a textual beast. They consist of academic treatises, novels, personal essays, biographies, a little philosophy, a film or two, and even poetry. They range over mythology, fiction, biology, wildlife studies, sociology, personal reminisce, tirade, journalism, propaganda, and even theory, particularly in what has become known in English departments as "animal studies." This is by no means meant to be an exhaustive literature survey of coyotes.

The Voice of the Coyote, by J. Frank Dobie (Curtis Publishing Company, 1947)
Hunters Horn, by Harriette Simpson Arnow (originally published 1949;
   Michigan University Press edition, 1997)
Big Woods: The Hunting Stories of William Faulkner (Random House, 1955)
The Savage Mind, by Claude Levi-Strauss (first appeared in French, 1962;
   English translation, Oxford University Press, 1966)
God's Dog: The North American Coyote, by Hope Ryden (Lyons and Burford, 1975)
The Wild Canids: Their Systematics, Behavioral Ecology, and Evolution, edited
   by M. W. Fox (Van Nostrand Reinhold Company, 1975)
Coyotes: Biology, Behavior, and Management, by Marc Bekoff (Academic
   Press, 1978)
Of Wolves and Men, by Barry Lopez (Scribners, 1978)
About Looking, by John Berger (Pantheon Books, 1980)

The Dixon Legend, by Solon Dixon (Strode Publishers, 1982)

Adam's Task: Calling Animals by Name, by Vicki Hearne (Alfred A. Knopf, 1987)

American Wildlife in Symbol and Story, edited by Angus K. Gillespie and Jay Mechling (University of Tennessee Press, 1987)

Woodrow's Trumpet, by Tim McLaurin (Down Home Press, 1989)

Meant to Be Wild: The Struggle to Save Endangered Species through Captive Breeding, by Jan DeBlieu (Fulcrum, 1991)

The Ninemile Wolves, by Rick Bass (Clark City Press, 1992)

A Coyote Reader, edited by William Bright (University of California Press, 1993)

The Crossing, by Cormac McCarthy (Random House, 1994)

Eastern Coyote: The Story of Its Success, by Gerry Parker (Nimbus, 1995)

Animals in the Fiction of Cormac McCarthy, by Wallis R. Sanborn III (McFarland and Company, 1996)

Another Country: Journeying toward the Cherokee Mountains, by Christopher Camuto (Henry Holt, 1997)

Heart and Bone: Living with Deer in America, by Richard Nelson (Alfred A. Knopf, 1997)

Never Outfoxed: The Hunting Life of Benjamin H. Hardaway III, by himself (Benjamin H. Hardaway III, 1997)

Aldo Leopold: His Life and Work, by Curt Meine (University of Wisconsin Press, 1998)

Cities of the Plain, by Cormac McCarthy (Random House, 1998)

Ecology of Fear: Los Angeles and the Imagination of Disaster, by Mike Davis (Henry Holt, 1998)

Trickster Makes This World: Mischief, Myth, and Art, by Lewis Hyde (Farrar, Straus and Giroux, 1998)

Killing Coyote: A Doug Hawes-Davis Documentary (Fund for Animals/High Plains Film, 2000)

A Language Older Than Words, by Derrick Jensen (Context Books, 2000)

Prodigal Summer, by Barbara Kingsolver (Harper Collins, 2000)

Aldo Leopold and the Ecological Conscience, edited by Richard L. Knight and Suzanne Riedel (Oxford University Press, 2002)

Animal Rites: American Culture, the Discourse of Species, and Posthumanist Theory, by Cary Wolfe (University of Chicago Press, 2003)

Hoagland on Nature: Essays, by Edward Hoagland (The Lyons Press, 2003)

Coyote: Seeking the Hunter in Our Midst, by Catherine Reid (Mariner Books, 2004)

Sick of Nature, by David Gessner (Dartmouth College Press, 2004)

Wolves and Honey: A Hidden History of the Natural World, by Susan Brind Morrow (Mariner Books, 2004)

Aliens in the Backyard, by John Leland (University of South Carolina Press, 2005)

The Old Way: A Story of the First People, by Elizabeth Marshall Thomas (Picador, 2006)

Where the Wild Animals Is Plentiful: Diary of an Alabama Fur Trader's Daughter, 1912 1914, by May Jordan, edited by Elisa Moore Baldwin (University of Alabama Press, 2006)

American Coyote: Still Wild at Heart, a film by Melissa Peabody (2008)

The Hidden Life of Deer: Lessons from the Natural World, by Elizabeth Marshall Thomas (Harper Collins, 2009)

Inside of a Dog: What Dogs See, Smell, and Know, by Alexandra Horowitz (Scribner, 2009)

The Coyote at the Kitchen Door: Living with Wildlife in Suburbia, by Stephen DeStefano (Harvard University Press, 2010)

Gray Ghosts and Red Rangers: American Hilltop Fox Chasing, by Thad Sitton (University of Texas Press, 2010)

Some We Love, Some We Hate, Some We Eat: Why It's So Hard to Think Straight about Animals, by Hal Herzog (Harper Perennial, 2010)

Weeds, by Richard Mabey (Harper Collins, 2010)

A Savage Empire, by Alan Axelrod (Thomas Dunne Books, 2011)

Year of the Pig, by Mark J. Hainds (University of Alabama Press, 2011)

The Forest Unseen: A Year's Watch in Nature, by David George Haskell (Viking, 2012)

Nature Wars: The Incredible Story of How Wildlife Comebacks Turned Backyards into Battlegrounds, by Jim Sterba (Crown, 2012)

The Complete Poems of James Dickey, edited by Ward Briggs (University of South Carolina Press, 2013)

Forgotten Grasslands of the South: Natural History and Conservation, by Reed F. Noss (Island Press, 2013)

The Secret World of Red Wolves: The Fight to Save North America's Other Wolf,
by T. Delene Beeland (UNC Press, 2013)

Coyote Summer, by Margo Solod (Brandylane Publishers, 2014)

Distant Neighbors: The Selected Letters of Wendell Berry and Gary Snyder,
edited by Chad Wigglesworth (Counterpoint, 2014)

The Margins of a Greater Wildness, by Richard Rankin (Willow Hill Press,
2014)